What Are We Waiting For?

Re-Imagining Advent for Time to Come

William H. Petersen

Church Publishing
NEW YORK

Church Publishing
19 East 34th Street
New York, NY 10016
www.churchpublishing.org

Cover design by Jennifer Kopec, 2Pug Design

Original cover A-Ω graphic by Martin Erspamer, OSB, a monk of St. Meinrad Archabbey, St. Meinrad, IN. Used with permission of the artist and Liturgy Training Publications, Chicago, IL.

Interior design and typesetting by Beth Oberholtzer Design

Library of Congress Cataloging-in-Publication Data

Names: Petersen, William Herbert, 1941– author.
Title: What are we waiting for? : re-imagining advent for time to come / William H. Petersen.
Description: New York, NY : Church Publishing, [2017] | Includes bibliographical references and index.
Identifiers: LCCN 2017018289 (print) | LCCN 2017031796 (ebook) | ISBN 9780898690385 (ebook) | ISBN 9780898690378 (pbk.)
Subjects: LCSH: Advent.
Classification: LCC BV40 (ebook) | LCC BV40 .P465 2017 (print) | DDC 263/.912—dc23
LC record available at https://lccn.loc.gov/2017018289

Printed in the United States of America

DEDICATION

To Priscilla,
for more than half-a-century and onwards,
tu mihi sola places.

Therefore, every scribe who has been trained for
the kingdom of heaven is like the master of a household
who brings out of his treasure what is new and what is old.

—Matthew 13:52

Contents

Acknowledgments

At a poignant moment in her commentary on Dante's *Divine Comedy*, Dorothy L. Sayers cites Charles Williams in *The Figure of Beatrice* relative to one's obligations to others: "For ever and ever derivation must be remembered, willingly praised, and ardently published before earth and heaven."[1] It is with a joyful sense of such obligation, then, that I undertake here to acknowledge great debts of derivation in all that has gone into the making of this book.

There are teachers long past such as Dante and F.D. Maurice as well as more recently passed, such as Massey H. Shepherd, Jr. and Norman Mealy who continue to influence thought and provide inspiration. There are present liturgical and ecumenical colleagues to whom continuing gratitude is due. Especially this is so to members of the Advent Project Seminar of the North American Academy of Liturgy, for whose continued collaboration I am deeply thankful. Also to be mentioned here for collegiality and counsel in this regard are members of the Council of Associated Parishes for Liturgy and Mission; the NAAL; the International Anglican Liturgical Consultation; the Consultation on Common Texts in North America; the English Language Liturgical Consultation internationally; and last but not least, *Societas Liturgica*.

Among those from one or another of these groups, several bear specific mention for enthusiastic and excellent contributions through the Advent Project Seminar: the Rev. Dr. Elise A. Feyerherm, Dr. Carol A. Doran, the

---

1. Dante, *The Divine Comedy:* 1 Hell, trans. and comm. by Dorothy L. Sayers (New York: Penguin Books, 1949), 166–167.

Rev. W. Richard Hamlin, Dr. Jill Burnett Comings, Dr. Laura E. Moore, the Rev. Dr. Suzanne Duchesne, and the Rev. Dr. Deborah Appler—these are noted at appropriate points in the text. Special thanks are due to the Rev. Dr. Gordon Lathrop for much-appreciated encouragement when I proposed establishing the Advent Project Seminar to the NAAL leadership. For technical assistance in the production of chant music attached to the text of Proper Prefaces, I am more than grateful to the Rev. John R. Clarke. Penultimately to be acknowledged with thanks are those parishes and congregations that have since 2005 seen the possibilities and are engaging this proposal for liturgical renewal with vigor.

And, finally, plaudits to my editor, Nancy Bryan of Church Publishing, not only for friendship and patience, but wise counsel in the forwarding of this work to publication. Reciprocity in the mentoring relationship is a wonderful thing for a teacher to acknowledge from a former student.

William H. Petersen

Advent over Seventy-Five Years: A Personal Reflection

Advent has fascinated me for a long time. Though there was never a time when I could remember not being taken by my parents to Sunday Holy Communion it was only when I became a young chorister (singing descant!) in a midwestern cathedral choir that I became truly aware of the season. It was particularly the music of Advent that, at first unconsciously, attracted me. Somehow I knew through the medium of song that this season was distinct with a purpose and quality all its own.

This intuition grew into knowledge as I matured enough to appropriate the meaning of the words that we were singing—such hymns as the yearning *Come, thou long expected Jesus*, or the militant *Lo, he comes with clouds descending*, or the clarion *Sleepers, wake!* or, finally, the cosmic perspective hauntingly expressed through *Creator of the stars of night*. The four-week brevity of the season seemed to be inversely proportional to the crucial weight of its message. Advent, then, was a season of expectation, of vision, of urgency and, running through all of these qualities to sum them up: *anticipation*. But anticipation of what? There seemed—perhaps inchoately at the time—to be a tension in this question.

In retrospect, that tension had something to do with the celebration of Christmas. Having been born a decade before mid-twentieth century, I can remember a pre-mall time when downtown department store fronts did not manifest holiday decorations or fill the length of their windows with the magic of moving dioramas illustrating *A Visit from St. Nicholas* until very late November. In fact, Santa Claus did not arrive in my home town until the very end of the Thanksgiving Day parade. The 1950s would, of course, change all that as we recovered from the rationing deprivations of World War II and the commercialization and lengthening of the Christmas season began in earnest. This, to be sure, was part of the tension around the question of what exactly was the *anticipation* involved in this season. The general cultural answer had begun to emerge: The time was anticipatory in the sense of a count-down to Christmas. It would, of course, grow into The Holidays that we now know—marked by a global Christmas Culture and featuring a protracted celebration of Christmas before the fact.

The other half of the tension, at least for a young chorister scaling down over those years to the tenor section of the choir, was provided by the fact that, in the churches observing a liturgical year, Advent was still held to be a penitential season of nearly Lenten proportions. So, on the one hand, we were being invited to early Christmas parties and, on the other, we were bending low in church under the implied threat of One who will come— *watch, for you don't know when!*—to be the Judge of our behavior. In those days even the decor of the churches featured little that was festive beyond the purple vestments and paraments, mitigated only by a fleeting splash of rose on the third Sunday. The now-ubiquitous (even in traditions not observing the liturgical year) Advent wreath was not present. Often transferred from a home devotional, the wreath only came into church venues during the latter decades of the twentieth century.

For the most part, a young person involved in both the culture and the church simply lived with the tension without critical speculation about who might prove to be the more lenient observer of one's deportment: the cultural icon who "sees you when you're sleeping . . . knows when you're awake" or the iconic Christ *Pantokrator*, the One coming "in glorious majesty to judge both the quick and the dead."[1] In any case, there the matter rested until long after the reality of the cultural icon faded away and, indeed, the believability of the second was challenged by the usual liberal arts and science courses of college years. There, however, the liturgical formation of early

---

1. Collect for the First Sunday of Advent, Book of Common Prayer (New York: The Church Pension Fund, 1928), 90. The prayer was composed for the first BCP of 1549. From the 1662 BCP through the 1928 version, a rubric directed that this prayer was to be said daily throughout the Advent season, keeping the character of the season (and, indeed, of the outcome of all time) very much in focus and, in this respect, standing over against the growing cultural alternative of a too early Christmas observance.

years served me well because I had the habit of going to church and singing in a choir regardless of what learning to think critically might be doing to the intellectually unsophisticated theological understanding with which I had come to college.

It was only in my seminary years, immediately following college, that the tensions surrounding the Advent season came back into my consciousness. It was there, too, that this consciousness expanded. In the context of a deeper theological education, it appeared that Advent was not primarily about the long-delayed, but perhaps imminent—at least at the point of death—Judge of one's individual life. Such an individualistic particularism was put into perspective by the consideration that Advent, at the verge of a new liturgical year, had principally to do with a more corporate vision of the Kingdom of Christ / Reign of God standing over against the ways of the world. Formation into such a vision could potentially form an attitude that might be carried into the entire liturgical year, qualifying and freeing it from being just another go-around or routine cycle.

These years, too, were an era when Vatican II was coming to a close and the reforms that followed it began to be effected. This was especially so in terms of a liturgical renewal that affected Christian traditions beyond the Roman Catholic. As one result of all this, the season of Advent in its general eschatological and corporate aspects emerged, incarnated for worshipers with a revised lectionary, and with penitential purple succeeded by a more blissful blue. How personally to interpret this development was largely the result of seminary studies and later a doctoral dissertation on F. D. Maurice (1805–1872), whose profound works of theological restatement provided a foundation for an eschatology not only adequate to our situation, but exactly applicable to the re-imagination of Advent as well.[2]

If these were some of the theological learnings conjoined to liturgical reforms, my formational appropriation of them came, once again, through music. Given past involvements, it seemed natural for me to enlist in the small liturgical choir initiated by our professor of church music during that

---

2. In particular, Maurice's *Kingdom of Christ* (1842) for its ecclesiology and his *Theological Essays* (1853) for their rethinking of the relationship between time and eternity stand out in this regard. Maurice's restatements were influential beyond his own Anglican tradition in making Christianity capable of facing the problems of the contemporary world without a retreat into authoritarianism or a flight into fundamentalism.

mid-sixties time (perhaps an incongruent development in the face of Berkeley's edgy free speech, fair housing, and anti-war protest era).[3] In any case, with our professor's leadership we produced an LP recording combining both venerable and new Advent music titled *O Come, O Come*. The result was a vision of Advent that, in congruence with the liturgical reforms, exhibited a focus on justice, peace, and the stewardship of creation as flowing from the liminality of the Reign of God / Kingdom of Christ. And it was this transformed vision of Advent that I carried with me from 1966 into the exercise of ordained ministry in the priesthood.

The next developments in a continuing engagement with Advent appear to have come at approximately twenty-year intervals. For instance, one of the more profoundly affecting pieces on our mid-sixties recording was R.B.Y. Scott's poem "O Day of God," set to the hauntingly beautiful tune *Llandaff*. Scott's composition set to various other tunes had appeared in the hymnals of many traditions subsequent to its 1937 composition. It was, therefore, a personal pleasure to be asked to write a commentary on the hymn and a biographical note on the author for *The Hymnal 1982 Companion*.[4] It was there, in an extensive exposition of this relatively concise hymn of five short verses, that the seeds of the present book were planted. Much more will be said, especially in Chapter 1, about what may be considered a highly significant hymn for the re-imagining of Advent. Yet, as indicated, the gestation was lengthy.

Two decades later, largely through conversations and studies associated with colleagues in the North American Academy of Liturgy, the International Anglican Liturgical Conference, and *Societas Liturgica*,[5] I was led to form the Advent Project Seminar in the NAAL in 2005. The NAAL members joining this seminar have not only been active in liturgical scholarship

---

3. It is understatement to say that Berkeley, California, in those days was quite a different context from the Midwest where I had grown up and gone to college! My seminary, of course, was the Church Divinity School of the Pacific and the leader of our song and recording, Professor Norman Mealy (1923–1987).

4. "O Day of God" appears in the Episcopal Church's *Hymnal 1982* at numbers 600 and 601 with the tunes, respectively, *Bellwoods* and *St. Michael*—neither of which, lamentably, captures the Advent quality of *Llandaff*.

5. NAAL is an ecumenical academy of liturgical theologians, as its name implies, principally from the United States and Canada; the International Anglican Liturgical Conference is an agency of the Anglican Consultative Council and functions as a kind of corporate liturgical officer for the Communion; *Societas Liturgica* is an ecumenical and international academy of liturgical theologians. These latter two organizations meet biennially.

for the presentation and interpretation of a re-imagined Advent, they have also worked to enlist congregations of various traditions in every region of the United States and from the Maritime Provinces to British Columbia in Canada for trial usage of an expanded and re-imagined season.[6] It has been our work also to provide resources both for education and for worship planning and use. We have also solicited evaluations from participating congregations in order to further refine this proposal for liturgical renewal.

And so we come to the present and the presentation of this book. It should be clear from the historical record that the season of Advent has already been subject to one profound re-imagining in the recent past. There have, of course, been other reforms of it previously and longer ago. These will also need to be addressed in the body of this book. As for this personal reflection itself, coming as it does out of a half-century of ordained ministry and seventy-five years of life in the Body of Christ, I hope it serves to give readers not only a bit of introduction to the author, but to lend at least *prima facie* evidence that the proposal for an expanded and re-imagined Advent is cogent and timely.

—William H. Petersen, January 2017
Week of Prayer for Christian Unity

---

6. In 2016 a congregation from Australia joined in trial usage, and some interest in the project is being expressed in South Africa. It will be interesting to follow whether and to what degree the experiment to re-imagine Advent can be helpful to churches of the Southern Hemisphere already challenged by many elements of the liturgical year tied directly to the natural seasons of the North.

Introduction

This book is intended for Christian congregations of all traditions that observe or are coming to follow a liturgical year in their worship. It seeks to reclaim for such worshiping assemblies a season that exhibits not only its own integrity,[1] but also an infusing quality for the annual round of the entire liturgical year from its very threshold as Advent begins a new year. Such a liminal approach to the season looks toward a liturgical renewal within the Christian community, one that holds significant consequences for its life and mission. To say this another way, of course, is simply to rehearse the words of a familiar hymn: The proposal of this book aims to help us "live more nearly as we pray."[2] The aim is a radical one in two senses: getting *to* the roots of Scripture and tradition and getting *at* the challenges facing the church in our age. The assumption, of course, is that worship is precisely where these elements meet both for individuals and for the entire Christian community.

Three questions, then, form the focus of this book. As it appears in the title, the first question might seem obvious. Upon reflection, however, it is ambiguous. In regard to Advent in the church year, the query might simply be understood as "What is it that *we* as church await, anticipate, or expect during the season?" This reading is, in fact, the primary question. Another reading, however, might hear the question as a clarion call to action. This

---

1. That is to say, a season observed for what it is in itself and not just as a brief ancillary period anticipating (or actually pre-celebrating) the even briefer twelve-day Christmas-to-Epiphany season that follows it .

2. John Keble (1792–1866): "New every morning is the love our waking and uprising prove; . . . [Lord] help us, this and everyday, to live more nearly as we pray." These are the first and final lines of a six-verse poem. Cf., *The Hymnal 1982* (New York: Church Hymnal, 1982), hymn 10.

possibility is directly suggested by the second half of the title. In other words, having re-imagined Advent, "How can we get going with its implementation, that is, how can we actualize it for the church's life and mission?" This is the third question at the heart of the matter. "But wait!" (I hear you ask.) "What's the second question?" It is an implied one that might already have suspiciously occurred in your mind: "Why do we *need* to re-imagine Advent?"

The response to these three questions will be addressed in a somewhat different order from this parsing of the title. Additionally, this book addresses a question about liturgical resources. The order of attending to the queries—with brief, not to say terse, preliminary responses to each one—is as follows:

Q: *What are we waiting for?* (Chapter 1).
R: The full manifestation of the Reign of God / Kingdom of Christ.

Q: *Why do we need to re-imagine Advent?* (Chapter 2)
R: The truncated season is eclipsed by the global Christmas Culture and the church's observance of Advent is liable to subversion by it.

Q: *What would be the shape and feel of such an Advent?* (Chapter 3)
R: Advent would start earlier and its observance would be a continuing exercise in the Gospel's counter-cultural redemptive message.

Q: *Are there any resources for observing such an Advent?* (Chapter 4)
R: Yes. The Advent Project Seminar has been at work on these with participating "trial use" congregations for over a decade.[3]

The book concludes with a fifth chapter addressing a number of pastoral and practical concerns for worshiping assemblies. Among these are: (1) What to do about the Advent wreath? (2) How might the annual steward-

---

3. Since 2005 the Advent Project has been a continuing seminar in the North American Academy of Liturgy. The NAAL is an ecumenical and inter-religious association of liturgical scholars who collaborate in research concerning public worship. Participating Advent Project congregations to date are from the Episcopal Church, the Evangelical Lutheran Church (US and Canada), the United Methodist Church, the Presbyterian Church USA, the Anglican Church of Canada, the United Church of Canada, and the Anglican Church of Australia. Participating congregations are represented in all major regions of the United States and Canada.

ship campaign mesh with an expanded Advent? (3) What can be done when All Saints' Sunday and Advent 1 coincide? (4) Where does church / Sunday school fit into all this? and (5) How can parishes / congregations participate in trial usage of an expanded season?

All of this constitutes a proposal for a liturgical renewal of the Advent season so that it does not continue to appear as the church's brief but late-coming preparation for the Christmas season—a season that the world has been celebrating with increasing anticipatory intensity each year for several months ahead of the holiday itself. In this proposal Advent is lengthened to seven weeks: from the first Sunday after All Saints' Day (November 1) through the Sunday before Christmas. An Advent in that mode shifts from an exclusively eschatological focus toward an initial incarnational one only at the very end of the season.

Besides reclaiming for the season an integrity of its own, an Advent focused on the Reign of God / Kingdom of Christ can become a season of formation for the entire liturgical year. To put these considerations in another way, Advent is not so much to be seen as a count-down to Christmas or even spiritually as a virtual pilgrimage to Bethlehem, but rather as a season that frames the entire round of the church year so that we may year by year grow further into living the full implications of the birth we celebrate at the commencement of the year's second season.

CHAPTER 1

Expectations

What Are We Waiting For in Advent?

Advent is, as it has always been, a season of waiting, expectation, and antic-ipation regardless of the changes that have re-imagined the season over the centuries. Its basic anticipatory nature holds true in either of the large his-torical traditions of Eastern and Western Christianity. While Advent is ven-erated as a kind of "winter Pascha" among the Orthodox,[1] it is not, however, regarded as the beginning of the new liturgical year. By contrast, in the West-ern Catholic tradition (and for all its derivative traditions once or several times removed), Advent stands as the inception of the new year. Whether it has been shorter or longer, Advent inaugurates the cycle of liturgical obser-vance moving from Christmas and Epiphany through Lent, Holy Week, and the Great Fifty Days of Easter to Pentecost and thence from that culminating feast to the long "green season" of ordinary Sundays, coming around again at last to Advent.

For all of this historical and contemporary congruency of mood there nevertheless remains the question already broached. It has to do not with the *mood*, but with the *message* of the season: *What* are we waiting for? A

---

1. The Eastern Church, of course, features the older six-week season even though their liturgi-cal year begins in September. For an exhibition of the Eastern emphasis on the season, especially with regard to eschatology, cf. Elise A. Feyerherm, "Wisdom from the East: Orthodox Advent as Winter Pascha," noted in *Proceedings* (Notre Dame, IN: Journal of the North American Academy of Liturgy, 2011), 11.

rather terse initial response to this question has already hinted at the conclusion: We are living in expectation of the full manifestation of the Reign of God / Kingdom of Christ. As liturgy is related to life and vice versa, there is here, then, an implicit claim that we await this result in and for the human community as we also anticipate it in and through our worship.[2] That is directly the crucial interplay in the search of our inquiry. Thus, as the focus of this chapter, the dimensions of our substantive question and its gist will be addressed through three subsidiary queries: (1) where would we look to discover the answer; (2) what about the *parousia* (second coming) problem; and (3) how can the substance of the season be succinctly explicated?

Finding Advent's Focus

Recently, as I was in the midst of an active retirement that still involved teaching a liturgics course for seminarians, my class had come to the topic of sanctifying time and an introduction to the liturgical year starting, of course, with Advent. At the outset of the session, I asked the seminarians to engage in a kind of thought experiment. Inviting them to suspend disbelief for a moment, I asked, "If you knew absolutely nothing about the season, where would you go to discover the focus and meaning of Advent?" Even though they were all adult learners, the instant response revealed a generation gap between instructor and students: "Google!" several shouted out amid the silent affirming nods of the rest of the class. When I had recovered some composure after laughing at my own naiveté in this age of instant information, I refined the question to "Where in an *ecclesial context* or a *church source* would you look?" After further conversation, it finally emerged that the Scriptures might provide such a source and, more particularly, the Scriptures as arranged for proclamation in worship by the readings of the church's lectionary for the Sundays

---

2. This interplay of liturgy and life has received significant reaffirmation in Stephen S. Wilbricht's *Rehearsing God's Just Kingdom: The Eucharistic Vision of Mark Searle* (Collegeville, MN: Liturgical Press, 2013). Searle emphasizes the formational potential of liturgy over time: "His aim is to demonstrate that, in all things liturgical, 'rehearsal' demands deep attentiveness, while the 'attitudes' practiced necessitate a willing surrender of self. If enacted with alert attentiveness and contemplative care, the liturgy itself becomes the revelation in our world of the 'justice of God.'" (35) Taken corporately this incarnates within the human community the flourishing intended by God and methodically explicated in the mustard seed or leaven analogies of Jesus's parables (respectively Matt. 13:31–32 or Luke 13:21) or Paul's analogy of leaven's effect within all the dough (1 Cor. 5:6 and Gal. 5:9).

of the season itself.[3] Leaving aside the controversies of the sixteenth century about the purpose and propriety of lectionaries, these Sunday-by-Sunday organizers of Bible readings are inextricably tied to the use of a liturgical calendar as they both support and exhibit the annual cycle of the ecclesial year.[4]

The Sunday and seasonal Scriptures, whether arranged for proclamation in public worship by the *Revised Common Lectionary* or the Roman Catholic *Ordo Lectionem Missae*, provide particular and appropriate portions of the story that inform and shape the very being and activity, the life and mission, of the Christian congregation as the eucharistic assembly. Charts of the two lectionaries with *préces* by the author for every reading may be found online at www.churchpublishing.org/whatarewewaitingfor.

So to this point in our query about where we might go to discover the meaning or focus of any particular Sunday or season, the lectionary stands out as the treasury to which we might have recourse in our quest. Two other factors ought here to be mentioned as foundational to how the lectionary thematically shapes and defines our worship. The first has to do with the reform that produced a three-year cycle of readings. In the Vatican II reform, a three-year lectionary was established with each year focused principally on readings from the synoptic Gospels of Matthew (Year A), Mark (Year B), and Luke (Year C), with the Gospel of John deployed as either supplemental or for particular seasonal interpretive purposes. Yet perhaps the most significant aspect of this more comprehensive provision for the proclamation of Scripture within the

---

3. There are, of course, two major lectionaries now in use: the *Ordo Lectionum Missae* (OLM) for the Roman Catholic Church globally and the *Revised Common Lectionary* (RCL) that is increasingly being adopted beyond the North American context by churches of other traditions. As explicated in Chapter 3 (cf. note 3), there is sufficient congruity between these two major lectionaries during the Advent season, whether longer or shorter, to posit a common understanding. This is particularly true for the Gospel and Epistle readings.

4. An excellent "Introduction" to lectionaries in general may be found at the outset of the Consultation on Common Texts twentieth anniversary annotated edition of *The Revised Common Lectionary* (Minneapolis: Fortress Press, 2012), ix–xxv. Also republished as an appendix in this edition is the instructive original "Introduction" to the Revised Common Lectionary (Appendix B, 185–206). Neither of these introductions, however, deal historically with the major rejection of any lectionary by the sixteenth-century Reformed or Radical Reformation traditions. This dissension (especially for English-speaking Christianity) was then rooted in what was considered by those traditions a distinction between human arrangement and divine inspiration in regard to Scripture. The growing acceptance of lectionary use in our own times, even among the heirs of those traditions or their derivatives, may simply reflect that (a) the issues of the sixteenth century are no longer ours and (b) the demands of our contemporary culture require the heuristic solution provided by such lectionaries for an understanding of life and mission.

Eucharist was the restoration of lections from the canon of Hebrew Scripture.[5] This development of the lectionary persistently calls to mind not only our Jewish roots as Christians, but our debt to that heritage within the People of God.

The second element of the liturgy that supports the lectionary as providing the thematic structure or focus to any particular Sunday celebration or continuing seasonal observance is to be found in the collects for the church year. These thematic prayers at once form a conclusion to the eucharistic assembly's Gathering Rite and the transition to the Liturgy of the Word.[6] While the actual structure of the 1979 Book of Common Prayer is not as clear about this pattern as it could be, the more recent *Evangelical Lutheran Worship 2006* clearly sets forth this pattern for eucharistic worship, showing the "Greeting" and "Prayer of the Day" (Collect) at the transitional point from Gathering to Word.[7] Furthermore, where the current prayer book shifted some of the ancient collects or provided new ones for the sake of a better match with the three-year lectionary,[8] *ELW 2006* provides three collects for each Sunday of the year so that the thematic prayer presages the

---

5. In prior lectionaries there were only vestiges of the fact that what the Nicene Creed calls "the Scriptures" (that is, the Old Testament books) were originally a fundamental part of readings for the Lord's Day. Having grown up with the 1928 Book of Common Prayer (in which only Epistle and Gospel readings for Sundays were provided), I remember how strange it appeared to me that "*For the Epistle*" on the "Sunday Next Before Advent" there appeared a reading from the prophet Jeremiah 23:5ff. Cranmer, of course, had retained this reading from the Sarum Rite as signaling an Advent emphasis: "Behold, the days come, saith the Lord, that I will raise unto David a Righteous Branch, and a King shall reign and prosper, and shall execute judgment and justice in the earth." The instance is singular and peculiar to Anglicanism (no such reading occurred in Sunday Roman lectionaries from the early Middle Ages onward), but also singularly important to the vestigial point being made here. Cf., Massey H. Shepherd, Jr., *The Oxford American Prayer Book Commentary* (New York: Oxford University Press, 1963), 225.

6. Originally, in fact, the Gathering Rite of the Eucharist may have consisted solely of the presider's greeting (*Dominus vobiscum*—The Lord be with you), the people's response, the *Oremus* (Let us pray) and the Collect as the thematic prayer of the day. A vestige of such a brief Gathering Rite can still be found in the BCP 1979 at the commencement of Ash Wednesday with the rubrical direction: *On this day, the Celebrant* [*sic*] *begins the liturgy with the Salutation and the Collect of the Day* (264).

7. *Evangelical Lutheran Worship* (Minneapolis: Augsburg-Fortress, 2006), is the commended (USA) and approved (Canada) liturgical book for the Evangelical Lutheran Church in those two countries. It clearly lays out the four-fold pattern with the particular elements of each portion at the beginning of the eucharistic section (92–94).

8. In the BCP 1928, for instance, the venerable collect for Advent 2 asking that we might "read, mark, learn, and inwardly digest" the Scriptures was moved in the BCP 1979 to the Sunday before the present last Sunday after Pentecost and an edited version of a collect from the Church of South India (about the prophets as messengers) was substituted as a better fit with that Sunday's readings and the theme of the season. Cf., Marion Hatchett, *Commentary on the American Prayer Book* (New York: Seabury Press, 1980), 166.

readings of a particular year's cycle even more directly. In any case, however, the Collect/Prayer of the Day serves its traditional function as a succinct thematic gateway to the readings in the Liturgy of the Word.

So, to reiterate the point of the discussion thus far, the major lectionaries along with the collects or prayers of the day in the liturgical year directly provide the source from which the meaning or focus of a particular Sunday or season can be discerned. Here, then, the singularly pressing question of Advent—"What are we waiting for?"—comes to the fore. To determine this focus or meaning, regardless of whether an expanded season of seven weeks or the present truncated four week period is under consideration, the lectionary becomes central.

For assessing the focus and meaning of Advent, then, it will be well to begin with the Gospel readings as providing the climactic moment for the Liturgy of the Word. In the presently predominant four-week season, the Gospels set for the first Sunday in the three-year cycle announce (Year A) that the Son of Man is coming unexpectedly (Matt. 13:36–55), so (Year B) be ready for you do not know the day (Mark 13:24–37), and, to put a fine point on it (Year C), Christ is coming in power and glory (Luke 21:25–36). According to the synoptic pattern of the cycle, then, by the second week we find the focus on John the Baptist taking up his mission to prophesy that the Kingdom of Heaven is near and that its appearance will bring salvation. In the third week this eschatological focus is made even more explicit by meeting the expectation created by his proclamation with the direct statement that Jesus is the Messiah, the One who will fulfill all this. At this point, then, we are three-fourths of the way through the season without a single reference to incarnation, preparation for the Nativity, much less the taking of a spiritual pilgrimage to Bethlehem.[9]

It is only in the last Sunday of Advent (coming only seven or, more often, fewer days before Christmas) that a transition toward incarnation, Nativity,

---

9. A chart of the readings with *precés* of their content for both the *OLM* and *RCL* may be found and downloaded at www.churchpublishing.org/whatarewewaitingfor. Here I have made the scriptural references explicit only in the first sentence. Anyone referencing the chart at this point will need to start with the readings for Advent 4, since the chart was created to set forth the lectionary in an expanded season of seven weeks—a point toward which the discussion is moving. Both the *OLM* and the *RCL* feature the same Gospel readings in these weeks (with only a variation of a few verses between them). In the penultimate week of Advent both lectionaries insert a Johannine reading for a Marcan one in order to emphasize the point that John the Baptist explicitly identifies Jesus as the Messiah.

or Bethlehem even begins to appear. The Gospel readings for that day focus in the cycle's order on: Joseph's espousal to Mary, the Annunciation, and the Visitation of Mary to her cousin Elizabeth, mother of John the Baptist. In the *RCL* these pre-Nativity readings are supported in that focus for two of the three years by substituting a Lukan canticle, the Song of Mary (*Magnificat*) for the Psalm. Keeping in mind that Mary is the archetypical symbol of the church as bearer of and witness to the Word of God, the *Magnificat* stands out in this liturgical setting as emphasizing and summarizing the implications during prior weeks of qualities associated with the salvation or vision of human flourishing inherent in the Reign of God / Kingdom of Christ.[10]

With that supporting note from the *Magnificat*, we may turn to the other lections of these four weeks to ascertain whether and to what degree they support the Gospel readings, defining in their singularly eschatological character the focus and meaning of the Advent season. A close reading of the *préces* composed for these online *OLM* and *RCL* lections clearly shows that they do so, whether taken from early Christian writings or the Hebrew prophets. The themes for these weeks prior to the end of Advent revolve around two poles. First, from the prophets comes proclamation of God's impending judgment in the world, coming as a cleansing agent from an heir to David's kingdom and resulting in a new day for God's creation, whether the vision is of the desert blooming or the Lord's glory revealed in the peaceable kingdom realized on God's holy mountain.[11] Second, from the Epistles comes also a call to "Rejoice!" as the day of God's judgment is identified with the disclosure of Jesus Christ in the world as the "root of Jesse" and,

---

10. Luke 1:45b–50, 53–54. The early Church accorded Mary the title of *Theotokos* (God-bearer), the Greek equivalent of the Latin West's *Mater Dei* (Mother of God). On the model of Mary, all Christians are called to be *theotokoi*, God-bearers. There are also in Luke's *Song of Mary* profound implications for our ecclesial mission: the showing of mercy, challenging the conceit of the proud, raising up the oppressed, feeding the hungry, and so on. In short, establishing restorative justice in this world as the world orders itself over against the Reign of God / Kingdom of Christ. It is small wonder, then, at the end of the day (literally in the evening office) that through the centuries the *Magnificat* has been the designated reminder of such mission as the transitional canticle between the two Scripture readings.

11. So for the prophets, Isaiah predominates with choice interjections from Jeremiah, Malachi, and Zephaniah (interestingly in this last case proclaiming that we should "Rejoice!" because God's just vengeance has been averted in favor of mercy—comforting news!). Between *OLM* and *RCL* there is only one variant during these weeks. It comes with the former inserting an Apocryphal word of consolation for Jerusalem from Baruch instead of Malachi's question about who can stand when God appears like a refiner's fire and a fuller's soap (a reading that at the least may induce listeners to hear in their heads a particular recitative from Handel's *Messiah*).

therefore, David's heir. Coupled with this emphasis is the petition, especially in Paul, that we (hearers both then and now) may be found blameless in this "day of our Lord Jesus Christ."[12]

Given the witness of the lectionary, then, there can be little doubt that the focus and meaning of the Advent season is principally and profoundly discovered in an emphasis on the culmination of what God has achieved "for us and for our salvation" (Nicene Creed) in the resurrection of Jesus Christ. From that point, in terms of the Gospel, the outcome is clear: the Reign of God / Kingdom of Christ is not only established, but it will overcome the depredations of the world. The eucharistic liturgy is not only a reminder of and witness to this for Christians, it is an anticipation in hope of its ultimate manifestation to all. Hence, as the antiphon/refrain for the hymn version of the canticle *Dignus es* succinctly states of every Eucharist: "This is the feast of victory for our God. Alleluia, alleluia, alleluia." But the canticle itself is even more evocative of the eschatological Advent focus at the beginning of the liturgical year:

Worthy is Christ, the Lamb who was slain,
whose blood set us free to be people of God. [*Antiphon*]

Blessing, honor, glory and might be to God
and the Lamb forever. Amen. [*Antiphon*]

For the Lamb who was slain has begun his reign.
Alleluia. [*Antiphon*][13]

Yet even given all this, there remains a question about whether an annual four-week Advent season is adequate to the task of providing the eschatological

---

12. For these three weeks, selections from early Pauline writings predominate with congruently thematic support from 2 Peter and the Epistle of James. Again, there are only small variations between *OLM* and *RCL* readings consisting of a few verses from otherwise identical books and/or chapters.

13. *The Hymnal 1982* (New York: Church Hymnal, 1982), hymns 416, 417. Verses 2 and 3 are omitted from this citation for brevity. The passage is from Revelation 5:12–13. In the BCP 1979 this passage as expanded by several preliminary verses forms Canticle 18 (93–94) and recommended twice per week for recitation after the NT reading for those who observe Daily Morning Prayer (cf. 144). Canticle 18 is also accorded musical settings in the *H82* at hymns S 261–266. In ELCA's *Evangelical Lutheran Worship* (Minneapolis: Augsburg Fortress, 2006), this canticle is featured as an alternate hymn of praise to the *Gloria in excelsis* in fully nine of the ten eucharistic settings provided and is frequently used by Lutheran congregations.

formation clearly envisioned by the thematic Sunday lectionary in that period. It is no secret that cultural forces and influences starting well before these few weeks impinge upon the time. There are also patterns and influences within the church that can lead all-too-often to ecclesial complicity with that now global "Christmas Culture." Consideration of these matters will be the focus of Chapter 2. For the present, suffice it to take notice of the fact and to suggest stepping back from the four weeks to take a larger perspective upon what the lectionary offers as a focus and emphasis for the three weeks prior to the short version of Advent.

During the long green season of "ordinary" time after the Feast of Pentecost, the Gospel readings in the three-year cycle tend to lead us around the Galilean countryside where, like his original hearers, we are invited to ponder Jesus's parables of the Reign of God / Kingdom of Christ. These considerations often follow upon or introduce evidential signs of healing and reconciliation characteristic of that Reign / Kingdom. There is, however, a distinct, not to say, sharp, change in the atmosphere provided by the lectionary after November 1.[14]

From the first Sunday after the Feast of All Saints, the lectionary begins dramatically to dwell not on likenesses of the Reign of God / Kingdom of Christ, but precisely on its powerful proximity. In these November weeks, the Gospel readings speak of a time of sorting out, of judgment, of Christ's appearing and sovereignty. Such themes are adumbrated or supported by the other readings.[15] The prophets provide us with alerts that God will "shake heaven and earth"; will raise up an heir to the line of David; and justice will abound. Pauline writings—aided and abetted by passages from Hebrews and Revelation—speak directly and urgently over these three weeks of the coming of Christ (and what to do in preparation for "the Day"); reminding

---

14. This can be discerned in attending to the lection *préces* provided for those three weeks in the online charts.

15. A comparison of the charts in the Appendix will disclose only minor differences between the *OLM* and *RCL* during these three weeks. The second readings are congruent between the two lectionaries, varying in a few cases by a verse or two. While the thematic emphasis of the first lessons is the same for *OLM* and *RCL*, the former employs two readings from the Apocrypha, Wisdom literature, and Daniel, where the latter depends more directly on the prophets. The comparative Psalms chart shows more variation, but certain themes stand out when in five out of nine possibilities, the two lectionaries exactly correspond. Ironically, the *RCL* begins the three-week period with an "expect a kingdom" canticle from the Apocrypha (Wisdom 6:17–20). In any case, where the correspondences are exact, the following themes abound: "the Lord is King" and has "made known his victory" and "shall reign forever" making for peace ("war to cease in all the world").

the community that we *have been* transferred into Christ's kingdom; and, as a sign of hope for the whole world, proclaiming Christ's reign over all things, disclosing him as the Alpha and Omega, the beginning and the end of a redeemed humanity in a renewed creation.[16]

It may be understatement in the face of such a barrage to say that this is scarcely business as usual. It is, to use a major theme of the Advent season, a wake-up call with maximum and persistent volume. In other words, the new "Day" is upon us, replete with the eschatological themes that will continue to characterize the season all the way until the final week of the Advent season. Here, then, is a *prima facie* case for seeing the entire seven-week period as an expanded Advent season. What might be the shape and feel of such a season is, as noticed previously, the focus of Chapter 3. Meanwhile, this discussion of "what are we waiting for?" in Advent, short or long, is intended to raise the suspicion that the season may need to be re-imagined. Directly addressing the need for such a re-imagination is the burden of Chapter 2.

For the present, it may be claimed that the longer rather than the shorter season provides over time a better formational opportunity. With its overarching and consistent lectionary focus on the Reign of God / Kingdom of Christ comes the possibility during an expanded Advent of a more conscious and conscientious entry into an eschatological mode of ecclesial life and mission. Precisely because it involves a shaping and sharpening of attitude and exercise—faith and work in that order—it may prove more effective than the well-intentioned, but often ineffective resolutions that people tend to make at the start of a new year.

In all this, as always, much will depend on how the season is observed and celebrated. For both people and presider, this will require much of our worship: attention in an Advent mode to prayer and preaching, to song and ceremony, from gathering to going out. But in everything there will be necessity to attend to the proclamation of God's story in such a way as to incorporate worshipers to the point that it becomes their story. To reiterate, then, the point of an expanded Advent is simple: to make the season we observe congruent with the lectionary we already have.

---

16. Note the tense of the referenced Colossians 1:13 verse from the reading (Col 1:11–20): We *have been,* instead of *will be* transferred into Christ's kingdom. This, of course, is a direct reference to baptism and also, of course, will form an important consideration for the next section concerning the *parousia.*

The Problem of the Parousia

Thus far the argument for undertaking an expanded Advent has focused on the lectionary that shapes this season of anticipation and expectation by asking "What are we waiting for?" The answer has consistently been "the Reign of God / Kingdom of Christ." Yet it might be objected that a preliminary question to *What?* is *Who are we waiting for?* And this question will refer us directly to what the New Testament calls the *parousia* (παρουσία)—the appearance of Christ in glory, to put it briefly. This, of course, was a highly pertinent question for the early Christian community founded upon their witness to Jesus's resurrection and the fact that he was with them now in a manner different from their previous experience.

In general terms of classical usage *parousia* carried the meaning of "presence" and, derivatively, of "appearance" as the first stage of a person's coming or advent. More technically, *parousia* developed into an official term for the visit of a person of high rank, especially of kings and emperors visiting a province.[17] Religiously, the term came to be expressive of the epiphany, appearance, or presence of a deity.[18] By the time of the Roman Empire the political and religious meanings were conflated as the divinity of the emperor was explicitly proclaimed. Though *parousia* is used in the New Testament along the entire range of its meanings, from everyday to technical, it not difficult to understand why in the vast majority of instances it refers to the appearance or manifestation to all of Christ in glory.[19] This anticipated fulfillment of the implications of the resurrection stands as direct challenge to Roman imperial politico-religious claims.[20]

There has, of course, been great debate in subsequent Christian history about when and how this will happen. The early Christian movement expected the *parousia* almost at once. The Marcan gospel, for instance, quotes

---

17. William F. Arndt and F. Wilbur Gingrich, *A Greek-English Lexicon of the New Testament and Other Early Christian Literature* (Chicago University Press, 1952), 635.

18. *The Interpreter's Dictionary of the Bible: An Illustrated Encyclopedia in Four Volumes* (Nashville: Abingdon Press, 1962), Vol. K–Q, 658.

19. Ibid., 658–659. It should be noted here that the term "second coming" as a synonym for *parousia* appears late, being first used by Justin Martyr (*ca* 100–*ca* 165) around mid-second century.

20. A profound study of this challenge is to be found in John Dominic Crossin, *God and Empire: Jesus Against Rome, Then and Now* (New York: Harper, 2007), particularly the chapters titled "Jesus and the Kingdom of God" (4) and "Apocalypse and the Pornography of Violence" (5).

Jesus's remark to his disciples, "Truly, I tell you, there are some standing here who will not taste death until the Kingdom of God has come with power" (Mark 9:1). Yet even in the early literature of the movement the "when" of such an expectation was qualified: "But about that day and hour no one knows, neither the angels of heaven, nor the Son, but only the Father" (Matt. 24:36). Subsequent history for Christians seems to be caught between these poles. In regard to the actual, that is, the operative presence of the Kingdom this has led to the apparently paradoxical expression "already but not yet." It is, nevertheless, the "how" of Christ's appearing as the full and final manifestation of God's reign that has provided for the exercise of great imagination, sometimes of vividly apocalyptic proportions, in both art and literature.

It is precisely at this juncture that the distinction between apocalyptic and eschatological vision must be applied and elucidated. Both, of course, involve the crucial element of judgment, that is, of a redress of injustice or oppression, a sorting out between good and evil, a cleaning up or restoration of creation, and, in short, to use a common phrase, "Kingdom come." Significantly, it is instructive to note that the word for judgment in Greek throughout the New Testament is *krisis* (κρίσις) from which, of course, we derive "crisis" and "critical."

Apocalypticism finds great opportunity for its expression in times of crisis and, in the face of crucial events, it offers critical solutions. The manner of apocalyptic art or literature is, however, one of disguise, principally because the situation addressed is extremely hostile or contradictory to the alternative it proposes. Scripturally, the first strategy of apocalyptic disguise is to change the time frame, to remove the situation from the threatening present so that its expression may more safely be viewed or heard. Then its meaning can be discreetly discerned by those to whom it is addressed and they can take comfort or warning as appropriate. So the situation may as for instance, in the Book of Daniel,[21] be removed to a reconstructed past; or, as in the Revelation to John (*nb*: Apocalypse), a reconfigured future.[22] In either case,

---

21. The Book of Daniel envisions a setting in the sixth century BCE Babylonian empire of Nebuchadnezzar during the Jewish exile, whereas dating of the book's composition (mid-second century BCE) indicates an apocalyptic judgment against the depredations of the then current Greco-Syrian Seleucid empire in the time of Antiochus IV Epiphanes in Judea and against the practice of Judaism.

22. John's Apocalypse envisions the coming (that is, future) cataclysmic downfall of the Roman Empire (rather thinly disgusied as a beast with seven horns, traditionally interpreted as the seven hills of Rome), to be replaced by the Reign of God / Kingdom of Christ. As history continued,

however, whether righteous or oppressed (or both), there is the hope or promise that the victims will be vindicated by God and enjoy a better future.

That "better future" will, of course, involve the vividly imagined destruction of the enemy, oppressor, or corrupted situation. And this is exactly where the major difficulty with apocalypticism begins to appear. The intensely encoded imagery of apocalyptic cannot escape the pattern of injustice that inspired it in the first place. A critical time, a "Day of Judgment," is imagined and it inevitably takes the form of violent retribution.[23] This grounding in fear, rather than love, results in projecting a violent aspect not only onto, but into the character of God. This represents the *moral* failure of apocalypticism.[24]

The *intellectual* failure of apocalyptic is to be found in the dead ends into which it tempts the literalistic adherents of its imagery. Much of apocalyptic imagery depends, for instance, upon a Ptolemaic three-tiered universe in which we no longer live. There have been several cosmological reconstructions (Copernican, Newtonian, Einsteinian) since the three-tiered, earth-centered scheme of the cosmos assumed in Scripture. Taking apocalyptic imagery literally, then, has serious implications for truth.

The *emotional* difficulty of apocalypticism completes the critique. With the apparent delay of the Kingdom or "second coming" there is the tendency to read apocalyptic passages of Scripture as indicative or, more often, predictive of current events, concluding that "the end is near!" This is the Millennialist alternative, so prevalent in American culture since the nineteenth century. Its problem is that the predicted date comes, but without cataclysmic conclusion. So the time is simply re-set as a concession to disappointment.

---

subsequent interpretations would re-define the target of that judgment. As late as the fifth century CE, nevertheless, St. Augustine's seminal work *The City of God* kept Rome as the focus of contrast and contradiction to Kingdom.

23. Such apocalypticism can be documented beyond Scripture through subsequent human history. Often its effects have been and are deleterious. Such violent retributive imagining has flourished, and continues to abound in the present at critical times of real or imagined threat, whether in secular or religious cultures. The fears at the root of apocalypticism are reflected, for instance, in popular culture, cf. especially, Robert Joustra and Alissa Wilkinson, *How to Survive the Apocalypse: Zombies, Cylons, Faith, and Politics at the End of the World* (Grand Rapids, MI: Eerdmans, 2016).

24. A wide-ranging and profound investigation of the anatomy of apocalyptic and its moral difficulties is to be found in John Dominic Crossan, *How to Read the Bible and Still Be a Christian* (New York: HarperOne, 2015). The subtitle exactly indicates the point being made: *Struggling with Divine Violence from Genesis through Revelation.*

Of more recent mint, but springing from the same impulse is the Rapturist alternative, holding that in the coming violent judgment and destruction of the world some (presumably the righteous) will be whisked away (raptured) to another place.[25] Here again, however, fear is at the root and brings violence when such an apocalyptic "end" is envisioned or realized. Judgment is transformed thereby into judmentalism. And this judgmentalism takes the all-too-frequent path so rife, not only in religious American culture, but general culture, of regarding justice as solely the process of making accusation, affixing blame, and exacting retribution.

So, then, a literalistic apocalypticism as part of the larger answer in regard to Advent's "What are we waiting for?" has been found morally, intellectually, and emotionally inadequate or misleading in nearly every respect. Is there any hope to be found in what was set forth above as the contrasting category of eschatology? A transition to such a discussion may be introduced through reference to a pointed offering titled "The Fist" by a widely acclaimed contemporary poet, Mary Oliver:

There are days
when the sun goes down
like a fist,
though of course

if you see anything
in the heavens
in this way
you had better get

your eyes checked
or, better still,
your diminished spirit.
The heavens

---

25. The "Rapture" culture is particularly exemplified in Tim LaHaye and Jerry B. Jenkins's widely popular and apocalyptic *Left Behind* novels. The best critique of this impulse is to be found in Lutheran biblical scholar Barbara Rossing's *The Rapture Exposed: The Message of Hope in the Book of Revelation* (Boulder, CO: Westview Press, 2004), especially her chapters on "Non-violence" (7); "Hijacking the Lamb—Addiction to Wrath and War" (9); and "Rapture in Reverse—God's Vision for Renewing the World" (10).

have no fist,
or wouldn't they have been
shaking it
for a thousand years now,

and even
longer than that,
at the dull brutish
ways of mankind—

heaven's own
creation?
Instead: such patience!
Such willingness

to let us continue!
To hear,
little by little,
the voices—

only, so far, in
pockets of the world—
suggesting
the possibilities

of peace?
Keep looking.
Behold, how the fist opens
with invitation.[26]

The movement of this poem's imagery goes from sunset to sunrise, while the moral direction is from violence to peace, during which the threat implied by the fist is transformed by that last word "invitation" into the presence of hope. The palpably Advent quality of the poem may thus aptly lead into a reflection on eschatology as over against apocalyptic in regard to the *parousia*.

---

26. "The Fist" from the volume *THIRST* by Mary Oliver (Boston: Beacon Press, 2006), 46–47, used herewith by permission of the Charlotte Sheedy Literary Agency, Inc.

To this point, the familiar term "second coming" has been assiduously and purposefully avoided in the discussion. It has already been noted that the term as a translation of *parousia* is late-coming and outside the canon of Scripture.[27] "Second coming" has the further impairment of implying that either or both the Kingdom and Jesus Christ were once with us, are now absent, but will—sooner or later—come back. If one reads—or more appropriately within the community of faith, prays—the Psalms on a regular basis, there will be found the constant insistence and assurance that "God reigns!" regardless of the oppressions of human existence or the depredations and atrocities of worldly powers and principalities throughout history into the present moment and beyond.[28] As another instance, long tradition in the church has compiled several magnificent verses from Paul's letters to the Corinthians and Romans to form the great Easter season canticle *Pascha nostrum*, which, if nothing else, celebrates the living Christ present to us as we live in him:

Christ being raised from the dead will never die again;*
    death no longer has dominion over him.
The death that he died, he died to sin, once for all;*
    but the life he lives, he lives to God.
So also consider yourselves dead to sin,*
    and alive to God in Jesus Christ our Lord. Alleluia.[29]

The final difficulty with "second coming" as translation for *parousia* is exemplified by its close association with the literalist appreciation and application of apocalyptic imagery. Apocalyptic purpose tends to ground itself in either a reconstructed past or a reconfigured future. As contrasted with apocalyptic, eschatology tends rather to find itself directed to the present and performing in a different mode. Eschatology, to be sure, is as focused on

---

27. *Cf.*, above note 19. It only appears when the "imminentist" interpretation in regard to either Jesus or the Kingdom has been apparently disappointed.

28. This direct affirmation appears as early as Psalm 2; continues in a very focused manner in the regnal Psalms from 95 to 100 (two of which retain the first words Latin title *Dominus regnavit*, literally, "The Lord rules"; and is explicitly sealed in the so-called "Hallel" Psalms (146–150) at the close of the book: "the Lord shall reign. . . throughout all generations" (Ps. 146:9). Citations from "Psalter," BCP 1979.

29. BCP 1979, 83.

"the end" and "judgment" as apocalyptic, but both its sphere of operation and its mood are quite distinct.

To explicate and justify such a two-fold claim, reference must be made to the contemporary renovation of eschatological theology. A succinct and insightful exhibition of that renewal is documented in Thomas Rausch's recent study *Eschatology, Liturgy, and Christology: Toward Recovery of an Eschatological Imagination*.[30] From the medieval period in Western Christian theology "the end" and matters of "judgment" have largely dealt with the "last things" (*eschata*) and been focused on individual believers, all of whom finally face "death, judgment, heaven, or hell."[31] This is in contrast to early Christian emphasis on the *eschaton*, that is, the Age to Come, or Day of God—the denouement, or end result, of history as it is affected by the Paschal Mystery or, more specifically, Christ's resurrection with all its implications for human flourishing and the renewal of creation itself. Following a chapter documenting this development, Rausch specifically addresses the renovation of our time in his sixth chapter, "Eschatology and Liturgy":

> As we have seen, the early Christians gave expression to their eschatological hope in Christ's triumphant return when they gathered as a community of the saints on Sunday, the first day of the week, to celebrate the Eucharist. They called out in prayer *Maranatha*, "Come, Lord Jesus," one of the church's oldest prayers, faced toward the east to await his return, and prayed for the coming of the kingdom in the Lord's prayer.[32]

In re-examining this ancient and profound connection between the *eschaton* and the Eucharist, there is more than delineation of a contemporary call to ecclesial repristinization or an anachronistic recreation of the early eccle-

---

30. Thomas J. Rausch, SJ, *op. cit.* (Collegeville, MN: Liturgical Press, 2012).

31. Though complex in cause, this theological development was enabled by Peter Lombard (*ca* 1100–1160) through his *Sententiarum Libri Quatuor*. In these four books (Trinity, Creation & Sin, Incarnation & Virtues, and Sacraments & Last Things) he provided for the organization of the subsequent theological enterprise. Even up to the present, works of systematic theology are arranged in Lombardian form. This ensured in Western theology that matters eschatological—the four last things—would come last. If, on the other hand, one were to suppose a systematic theology in an early Church or Eastern Orthodox manner, it might properly begin with consideration of the *Eschaton* because that would directly affect whatever was to be said about God, the creation, *etc.*, and not simply be relegated to a final chapter.

32. Ibid., 123. This is the opening paragraph of the chapter.

sial situation.[33] Building from the growing theological realization that Christianity for our age and in time to come needs to recover such a vibrant expectation in worship precisely for the sake of participating in the *missio Dei*, God's mission in the world. Such a recovery of eschatological imagination is a direct implication of liturgical renewal. To put it another way, when worship loses its eschatological focus it is disabled from vivifying the true life of the church and, through that, from inspiring authentic mission in service of the Reign of God / Kingdom of Christ. Rausch makes an explicit conclusion to the possibilities for a recovered eschatological imagination at the heart of such a liturgical renewal:

> When the liturgy is done well, with presiders drawing the assembly into the presence of the holy, and the assembly is united in prayer, praise, and contemplation of Christ's sacrifice, the liturgy can be truly transformative. At the table we become one family. The future that God has in store for us is already breaking into the present. The risen Christ unites himself to us, gathering us in his name, incorporating us into his Paschal mystery, filling us with his Spirit, and making us his body for the world.[34]

A major part of the making of these connections comes as a gift from Eastern Orthodoxy to a previously impoverished eschatology of Western Christianity. The theological contributions of Alexander Schmemann (1921–1983) continue to be fruitful both in showing that Eastern liturgy has conserved its eschatological emphasis and in aiding Western Christianity in recovering a larger eschatological imagination. Explicated in Schmemann's *For the Life of the World*, the eschatological heart of Sunday—the eighth day, the day of the resurrection and renewing of creation—is at the center of liturgical consciousness on that day.[35] Through the liturgy, then, as the meeting place between God's eternity and our time comes the energizing source for the church's participation in the divine mission implied by Schmemann's title: "for the life of the world."

---

33. That kind of antiquarianism has already led many in a so-called post-Christian era to regard the Church merely as a kind of "society for the preservation of quaint anachronisms."

34. Ibid., 139–140.

35. Cf., especially 50. The full title of the work is instructive for both the eschatological and missional point being made here: *For the Life of the World: Sacraments and Orthodoxy*, 2nd ed. (Crestwood, New York: St Vladimir's Seminary Press, 1973).

Two matters springing from these considerations can bring this discussion of *parousia* to a close. The first is that the eschatological approach to those equivalencies among *the end* or *Day of God* or *appearance of Christ* is rooted in love rather than in the fear that seems so foundational to apocalyptic. In other words, it is God's love that provides not only the basis but the motivation in issues of ultimacy. For Christians, God has acted decisively in Jesus Christ for the redemption and salvation of the world and will bring that initiative to full manifestation and effect. Divine love has exhibited not only the lengths to which it will go "for us and for our salvation,"[36] but also has given the means whereby the human community may flourish here and now, and come to fulfillment. Those are the brackets within which the present of any and all generations exist and the method by which, as previously noted, such destruction, dissolution, and death as mark history can be met and overcome.

This Alpha-and-Omega, such a beginning and end, that creates the frame within which we live brings us directly to the second subject prior to closure of the *parousia* problem discussion, namely, *time* and its critical component *judgment*. A second contrast between the characteristics of apocalyptic and eschatology was indicated by the imagery of apocalyptic rooted either in the past or projected upon the future. It was proposed that eschatology in contrast to apocalyptic is focused in the present. That claim now requires some nuancing. The eschatological vision is grounded in the characteristic of divinity that is called *eternity*. In contrast to a creation that exists within a framework of time and creatures that are certainly subject to the succession of life events occuring within a temporal sequence, God's eternity is not only qualitatively different from time, but is capable of engaging the temporal sequence constantly or at any given point. One image of this eternity is as a vertical element intersecting the temporal sequence (conceived as a horizontal line) at any and all points.

Part of the diminishment of the eschatological element in the liturgy of Western Christianity stems from the gradual but palpable theological modification in the concept of eternity that began in the scholastic Middle Ages and, ironically, reached it strongest expression in the nineteenth century. Reflection upon the concept of eternity began to be set forth on the

---

36. This phrase of the Nicene Creed focused on the second person of the Trinity refers directly, of course, to the missio Dei or divine mission initiated by the incarnation.

basis of time, coming finally to the result that eternity was conceived as time extended indefinitely.[37] There is neither space nor time within this discussion further to delineate the anatomy of this development in Western theology, but the irony is that it reached its full expression just at the moment when Christendom experienced its own denouement. This was effected by three things: the revolutions that marked the end of the eighteenth century in Europe and America; their continuing social, political, and economic challenges during the nineteenth century, and the concluding demise of Christendom in the catastrophe of the Great War of 1914–1918.[38]

All of this gave cause, of course, for the theological restatement, liturgical renewal, and ecumenical rapprochement incumbent upon the churches in the face of that massive change of circumstance for their life and mission in the twenty-first century and beyond. A major piece of the necessary theological restatement has been reconceiving time and eternity and their relationship. Such rethinking has both influenced and been influenced by elements of liturgical renewal. As liturgical theologian Lizette Larson-Miller has observed of the resultant situation:

> Putting these pieces together—theologies of time, consumerism, and the potential impact upon both of our practice of living the liturgical year— may give us insights into how much this cultural impact has changed our understanding of time, especially within the liturgical reformations of the past fifty years.[39]

37. Other traditions have their exponents of the challenge to this development that began in the nineteenth century, but for Anglicans, indeed for much of subsequent English-speaking theology, it was F. D. Maurice (1805–1872) who began the reappropriation and restatement of a more early-Church understanding of eternity as qualitatively different from time and not, therefore, to be conceived as time extended indefinitely. Cf., especially "On Eternal Life and Eternal Death" the concluding chapter of his 1853 *Theological Essays* (New York: Harper & Brothers, 1957). So prevalent was the challenged theological opinion that Maurice was summarily dismissed from his professorships at King's College, London, for "heresy." (The actual euphemistic charge was teaching calculated "to disturb the minds of young theological students.")

38. The three principal revolutions, of course, were the American, the French, and the Industrial, to which must be added the Scientific—both following in their wake as well as influencing them. In regard to America, it has taken the longer time, a Second World War, and the terroristic vengeance of a post-colonial world for American culture to realize the fact that Christendom ended with World War I. In some ways, of course, the denial of its demise persists in various aspects or expressions of American culture.

39. Lizette Larson-Miller, "Consuming Time," in *Worship* (Collegeville, MN: Liturgical Press), vol. 88, no. 6, November 2014, 528.

These in turn have modified the terms by which Christians engage (or not) in dialogue and—often through mutually appropriated elements of liturgical renewal—action with regard to the unity of the church, commonly called ecumenism.

This triply-interrelated pattern for contemporary Christianity in the face of an awareness of global cultures and an increasingly secularized world represents an engagement with time made explicit through what is termed "history." This course of rapprochement, restatement, and renewal stands, however, in sharp contrast to countervailing forces reacting to the appearance and continuance of the contemporary situation. These may be clearly perceived in the temptation to disengagement from history represented by ecclesial authoritarianism whether it be represented through defensive polities, Scriptural and/or doctrinal fundamentalism, debilitating liturgical nostalgia or, indeed, a toxic admixture of all three impulses.

So how might all these considerations relate to the subject at hand, that is, the renewal of an eschatological ecclesial consciousness or, more comprehensively, imagination? To this point the eschatological emphasis of the readings appointed for the Liturgy of the Word during Advent, whether shorter or longer, have been explicated. Now the Liturgy of the Table comes more directly to the fore. It is precisely here that the engagement of Christian faith with history becomes paramount, but also the Christian hope for the transformation of history comes into clear expression.

In a recent aptly-titled study, *Remembering the Future: The Experience of Time in Jewish and Christian Liturgy*, Emma O'Donnell brings her Jewish heritage and Christian experience to good effect through a profound exhibition of a claim made in the preceding paragraph regarding both the valuation of time and the transformation of history. While careful to keep in mind the essential distinction between Jewish and Christian faith,[40] O'Donnell sets out the connection in liturgy between memory and hope, emphasizing the mutual impact of one upon the other:

---

40. "For Judaism, the final redemptive vision is of a messianic future yet to come. In contrast, the Christian eschatological vision is considered to be already partially inaugurated, growing out of the tension between the redemption already brought about by Christ and the fullness of the kingdom yet to come." O'Donnell, *Remembering the Future* (Collegeville, MN: Liturgical Press, 2015), 10.

This book examines the *experience* of time in liturgy, and, in doing so, addresses the existential human condition of being located in time and the fundamental awareness of time as it is informed by religious tradition and practice.

Jewish and Christian narratives of the religiously envisioned past and future are embodied liturgically, and this book charts the ways that liturgical communities perform the temporal orientation of the religious tradition, clothing themselves in the memory and hope embedded in their narratives. It argues that the ritual enactment of collective religious memory and hope evokes a unique landscape of time, the contours of which are determined by the ritually remembered past and the anticipated eschatological future.[41]

Her emphasis in all this, however, is to notice what occurs when these two aspects of liturgy are juxtaposed in the event. The landscape of experienced time is itself transformed and as a result "memory is eschatological and hope remembers." O'Donnell explicates this point through her discussion and application of insights from a wide range of theological luminaries, among them Schmemann, Hans Urs von Balthasar, Joseph Ratzinger, Patrick Regan, and Louis-Marie Chauvet.

Schmemann, as already hinted, finds in the Eucharist that time is taken up into the eschatological nature of the church, lifted from the monotonous (not to say, deadly) chronology of profane time into sacred time.[42] For von Balthasar, the reality of time has been transformed but not destroyed in the process of its redemption by Christ, as O'Donnell elucidates his work:

> In fact, the eternal is present in this human life and in each of its moments, in a manner never realized before or afterwards, not as what is timelessly valid (the "idea"), but as that which occurs here and now. The kingdom of God is eternal, but it is not an abstract concept of timelessness. It "occurs here and now"; its presence is active, and its action is in this very time.[43]

---

41. Ibid., x.

42. Ibid., 134. Here she is drawing principally upon Schmemann's *Introduction to Liturgical Theology* (Crestwood, NY: St Vladimir's Seminary Press, 1966).

43. Ibid., 132. Her citation is taken from von Balthasar, *The Glory of the Lord: A Theologial Asesthetics*, vol. 7, *Theology: The New Covenant*, trans. Brian McNeil (San Francisco: Ignatius Press, 1989), 167. We have met this approach already in F. D. Maurice (*supra*, no. 37) and O'Donnell extends the line of recovery in English-speaking theology by noting here the similar contribution of New Testament scholar C. H. Dodd (1884–1973) in articulating the concept of such a "realized eschatology" set forth especially in his *History of the Gospel* (1937).

Abbot Patrick Regan's contribution in this regard directly refers to the Holy Spirit's presence in the liturgy as engaged by the worship community:

> The pneumatological aspect of ritual is above all qualitative and attitudinal. It is sensed in the wholeness, fullness and density of the entire celebration. It is evident when speech and gesture, movement and song are complete, fluid, rhythmic and concentrated not truncated, dangling, diffused and thin. This can happen only when those who celebrate transcend the dislocations of time, space and mind inherent in social structure, and enter the world of homology, the world of the Spirit, in which everything mutually indwells and points to everything else.[44]

Such a perspective is fully consonant with liturgical theologian Louis Marie-Chauvet's insights as explicated in his *Symbol and Sacrifice*. In referring to the fullness of such *parousia* effected by the Spirit, Chauvet recalls that the oldest eucharistic anaphoras "show, in the recalling—the *anamnesis*—the *second coming* of the Lord Jesus, as well as of his death and resurrection, the Christian memory is eschatological, it is memory of the future."[45]

As emphasized by the subtitle of her work, O'Donnell expands this perspective in a subsequent introductory paragraph indicating the tradition upon which Chauvet's statement rests:

> In the temporal landscape of both Jewish and Christian liturgies time is experienced as multidimensional; memory is eschatological and hope remembers. Hope, as the anticipation of a religiously envisioned future, engages the remembered past and takes from it promises for the future. It sees God's intervention in history, in time, to be a promise for the "future history." Memory speaks to hope and hope speaks to memory. This, in other words, is eschatological memory; this is remembering the future.[46]

From the outset, however, O'Donnell lets Joseph Ratzinger's *The Spirit of the Liturgy* frame the discussion of time and eternity met in the eschatological element of worship: "The immediate event—the liturgy—makes

44. Ibid., 168. O'Donnell is citing from Regan's "Pneumatological and Eschatological Aspects of Liturgical Celebration," in *Worship*, 54:4 (1977), 350.

45. Louis-Marie Chauvet, *Symbol and Sacrament: A Sacramental Reinterpretation of Christian Existence* (Collegeville, MN: Liturgical Press 1995), 239. Cited in O'Donnell, x.

46. Ibid., xi.

sense and has a meaning for our lives only because it contains the other two dimensions. Past, present, and future interpenetrate and touch upon eternity."[47] Or, to reverse this perspective without in the least altering, but rather enhancing, the point under discussion, in the liturgy *eternity* touches upon the past, present, and future.

The exact locus of this meeting, furthermore, is best explicated by the eschatological recovery featured at the heart of nearly every contemporary Great Thanksgiving in the Table portion of the liturgy. At midpoint of the presider's prayer the worshiping assembly is invited to interject an acclamation that is succinctly but effectively articulated:

Christ *has* died.		We *remember* his death.
Christ *is* risen.	**or**	We *proclaim* his resurrection
Christ *will* come again.		We *await* his coming in glory.[48]

The verbs in these acclamations are purposely italicized here precisely to draw attention to the in-folding of the past and the future into an eschatological present at this critical juncture of the Great Thanksgiving. Originally received as a welcome insertion in the otherwise long oration (literally) of the presider, over time the acclamation can serve not only to give voice to the assembly, but as the people's own ratification and appropriation of God's transformation of history by what Christ has done, is doing, and will bring to completion—thus the acclamation is the Body of Christ recognizing itself as such and entering into the *missio Dei* for the world.

Such an approach may also enable over time further formation into an eschatological imagination by recovering that aspect in the brackets provided to the central acclamation of the Great Thanksgiving. The first of these is, of

---

47. Ibid., 3. Cf. Ratzinger, *The Spirit of the Liturgy* (San Francisco, Ignatius Press, 2000), 60.

48. While the citation is from BCP 1979, 363 and 368, in the Lutheran *ELW* (2006) only the first of the two for all ten of its Holy Communion settings is used; the Presbyterian *Book of Common Worship* (1993), while providing four congruent alternative acclamations, prefers the first formulation in six of its nine Great Thanksgivings; and the United Methodist *Book of Worship* (1992) uses the first exclusively for all seasonal Great Thanksgivings including those in ordinary time. All of these are derived from the revision of the Roman Rite following Vatican II. In the current *Roman Missal* (3rd ed., English trans., 2011), the first alternative acclamation disappears in favor of "We proclaim your death, O Lord, and profess your resurrection until you come again." The second acclamation shown above is featured as an alternative to the first where such exist among the traditions noted. It is derived as the people's acclamation from the Orthodox anaphora of St. Basil.

course, the conclusion of the *Sanctus* at the beginning as it captures this immediacy in affirming of Christ "Blessed is the One who comes in the name of the Lord." The second is provided by the general recitation of the Lord's Prayer immediately following the great "Amen" at the conclusion of the Thanksgiving: after the address, the first petition setting the context of the entire prayer is "your kingdom come, your will be done, on earth as in heaven."

As time and history are, then, transformed in this eschatological vision of Christ's *parousia*, so, too, is its critical aspect, namely, the quality of judgment attached to it. This also forms a part of the Advent question "What are we waiting for?" The tendency of apocalyptic to discover divine judgment through cataclysmic events or timetables of disaster tends not only to be modified, but, indeed, moderated by the eschatological theological approach here set forth. Judgment in the eschatological imagination tends to be located in the consistency of the divine love and faithfulness as over against an occasional warning intervention culminating in the vision of a fearful, not to say cataclysmic, final judgment.[49] In other words, judgment in the eschatologial vision is built into the entire fabric of the cosmos as well as the historical process from creation through redemption to salvation and is not simply postponed to the end.

Such an approach is chiefly exhibited in the Wisdom tradition and, in particular, Psalm 119, far and away the longest of the Psalter. Originally an extended acrostic of twenty-two sections having eight verses, each of a particular set beginning with a letter of the Hebrew alphabet in succession, there are a total of one hundred seventy-six verses. This song is a persistent meditation on the goodness and justice of God's judgments as they form not only the fabric of the world, but the formational fiber of life for any and all who would live rightly and consequences for any and all who do not. Though any number of verses from this extensive psalm might be cited in support of these claims, only a few will have to suffice here. The context is the psalm's constant one of praise that at once sets itself in a receptive mode of formation and also recognizes the futility of evil and its ultimate frustration. Thus:

---

49. This latter became so prevalent in Western Christianity when the eschaton was diminished to the *eschata* of death, judgment, heaven, and hell (*vide supra*, discussion of Rausch, 16 and n. 31) that the dreadful Day of God was not only applied to the general end, but to individual ends with the *Dies irae* (Day of wrath) in funeral masses. Here the overwhelming picture conflagration— "heaven and earth in ashes burning"—on the Day of Judgment is moderated only by a faint final plea for mercy. In the event, we may be grateful for composers like Fauré who added a gloriously redeeming *Pie Jesu* to their requiems at this point.

89 O LORD, your word is everlasting;*
     it stands firm in the heavens.

90 Your faithfulness remains from one generation to another; *
     you established the earth, and it abides.

91 By your decree these continue to this day,*
     for all things are your servants.

108 Accept, O LORD, the willing tribute of my lips,*
      and teach me your judgments.

118 You spurn all who stray from your statutes;*
      their deceitfulness is in vain.

161 Rulers have persecuted me without a cause,*
      but my heart stands in awe of your word.

164 Seven times a day do I praise you,*
      because of your righteous judgments.[50]

As this approach is so construed, divine judgment is a constant rooted in God's faithfulness and love. Those who, for whatever ends or reasons, set themselves over against the common good or the flourishing of the human community can only experience God's judgment as a consequence of their opposition rather than as a retributive divine punishment, presently or at some future date. Although, as indicated, this approach is rooted in the Wisdom tradition, it is at the same time not unlike the Deuteronmic tradition in which Moses sets out the divine condition of moral choice and its consequences: " . . . I have set before you life and death, blessings and curses. Choose life that you and your descendants may live, loving the LORD your God . . . ."[51] Much in that regard, however, depends upon whether the attached "curses" are seen as consequences or as punishments.[52]

The choice between eschatological and apocalyptic constructions of judgment in relation to the *parousia* continues, of course, into the New Testament.

---

50. Verses indicated from Psalm 119 set for recitation and cited from BCP 1979, *passim* 770–777.

51. Deuteronomy 30:19–20 (NRSV).

52. Sorting these alternatives out in regard to what he calls "God's great clean-up of the world" (judgment) is the burden of much of John Dominic Crossan's *How To Read The Bible and Still Be A Christian* and, for the present, it needs only be noted that the Deuteronomic strain throughout Scripture is weighed in the balance and found wanting.

On the one hand, for instance, is the vision set forth just before the passion and at the end of Jesus's teaching ministry in Matthew's Gospel. Here the vision of the Great Assize or Day of Judgment when "the Son of Man comes in his glory" results in a kind of Deuteronomic divide where those who have recognized Christ in their fellow human beings and acted accordingly (the sheep) enter into eternal life and those who have not so lived (the goats) receive the consequence of eternal death.[53] There is also in the New Testament, on the other hand, what may be termed the more invitational, consequential eschatological alternative construction. This may be seen, for instance, in the Johannine Gospel where we find, perhaps surprisingly, Jesus disclaiming a final judgmental role in the same time frame as the Matthean Gospel (that is, just before the Passover in the transition to the Passion narrative):

> Then Jesus cried aloud: "Whoever believes in me believes not in me but in him who sent me. And whoever sees me sees him who sent me. I have come as light into the world, so that everyone who believes in me should not remain in the darkness. *I do not judge anyone who hears my words and does not keep them, for I came not to judge the world, but to save the world.* The one who rejects me and does not receive my word has a judge; on the last day the word that I have spoken will serve as judge, for I have not spoken on my own, but the Father who sent me has himself given me a commandment about what to say and what to speak. And I know that his commandment is eternal life. What I speak, therefore, I speak just as the Father has told me."[54]

By what criterion do we sort out the stark contrast provided by these two alternatives? Here we can be aided by a principle of venerable standing, namely, that Christ is the criterion of the Scriptures. As is so often the case, the long tradition provides a Latin slogan for this axiom of interpretation, in this case *Christus norma normans normata*, that is, Christ is the standard that regulates what is to be taken as authoritative. John Dominic Crossan excellently brings out the implications of this principle in his interpretation of the icon titled *Christ Pantokrator*—an icon important to the vision of Christ's *parousia* in glory.

---

53. The imagery of Matthew 25:31–49 is vivid and, of course, is meant literally to scare the hell out of the reader/hearer. But again the presence of the "threat" or "fear" motif so typical of apocalyptic predominates.

54. John 12:44–50 (NRSV). Emphasis added.

As in all such Eastern icons, frescoes, or mosaics of Christ, his right hand is raised in an authoritative teaching gesture, with his fingers separated into a twosome and a threesome to connote Christian faith in the two natures of Christ and the three persons of the Trinity. As usual, he holds a book in his left hand. But he is not reading the book—it is not even open, but securely closed and tightly clasped.

Christ does not read the Bible, the New Testament, or the Gospel. He is the norm of the Bible, the criterion of the New Testament, the incarnation of the Gospel. That is how we Christians decide between a violent and a nonviolent God in the Bible, New Testament, or Gospel. The person, not the book, and the life, not the text, are decisive and constitutive for us.[55]

So, then, while the "when" of the full manifestation of the Reign of God / Kingdom of Christ must always remain God's business, the mode of its Advent must be an eschatological one characterized by a nonviolence such as is exhibited in the person and work of Jesus Christ. The implication is singularly important for us in the meanwhile as time and history are in-folded into the liturgy of the eucharistic assembly in general and, in particular, of the worshiping community formed by the lectionary of the Advent season. Through these things an eschatological imagination is to be formed in us, not only for the season, but to be carried into the new liturgical year. And this has the weight not just of a pious new year's resolution, but, rather, the crucial re-valuation of absolutely everything.

In yet another essay into the interpretation of the historical Jesus who has turned out to be *the* criterion, Crossan investigates the distinction between the Kingdom that John the Baptist announced as *imminent* with the Kingdom that Jesus proclaimed as *present*—a distinction very much to the point of what we might be awaiting in the Advent season. That distinction involved what we have in our times come to call a paradigm shift between John and Jesus in regard to eschatological expectation. Thus Crossan:

You have been waiting for God, [Jesus] said, while God has been waiting for you. No wonder nothing is happening. You want God's intervention, he said, while God wants your collaboration. *God's kingdom is here, but only*

---

55. Crossan, *God and Empire*, 95. The literal translation of the Latin slogan, Christ the norm that norms the normal things, can appear confusingly redundant, which is why I have paraphrased it in the paragraph preceding the citation.

insofar as you accept it, enter it, live it, and thereby establish it. That is the only possible interpretation that does not render Jesus's claim of the kingdom's presence a bad and cruel joke. He is announcing, in other words, not a realized, but a realizable *eschaton* or, better, a *collaborative eschaton*. The Great Divine Cleanup will not happen without God, but neither will it happen without us. It is about a divine-and-human collaboration and not about a divine-only intervention.[56]

Advent's Substance Succinctly Stated

In this chapter we have been examining the question of what exactly we are waiting for in the season of Advent. Our anticipation and expectation have been examined first from the substance to be found as the lectionary forms a particular emphasis and themes for the season. That substance has been set forth as overwhelmingly eschatological with an incarnational focus coming only at the very end of the season as a transition to Christmas. In discovering what the focus on the *eschaton* might mean, it was necessary—at some length and depth—to consider the problem of the *parousia*. Through that investigation several matters of importance to our overall question were discovered.

The primary one of course, for Christians, is the general equivalence among such terms as come before us in the Advent lectionary, for example, Day of God, Judgment Day, Day of our Lord Jesus Christ, and the *parousia* of Christ. Second, attention was paid to significant distinctions between apocalyptic and eschatological genres. These revealed, respectively, differences about time (calculable or not?), history (past, future, or present?), mood (dire or hopeful?), judgment (occasional, postponed, or continuing?), and foundational premises (fear or love?). In the process of this examination our focus has largely been upon the second half of the normative Sunday liturgy centered on Table. Here it was revealed that the general recovery and renewal of eschatology since the advent of the contemporary world has profoundly affected the understanding of Christ's *parousia* both as it infuses our worship and also energizes us for collaboration with the *missio Dei*, that is,

56. Crossan, *The Power of Parable: How Fiction by Jesus Became Fiction about Jesus* (New York: HarperOne, 2012), 127. All italics are Crossan's.

within and as agents of the Reign of God / Kingdom of Christ for the sake of the world.

Over fifty years ago, as I indicated in the Foreword to this study, I was captivated by a poem that seemed to bring together all that Advent had come to mean to that time and, subsequently, also became the inspiration for pursuing all that has been unpacked and explicated in this chapter.[57] The poem composed by R.B.Y. Scott in 1937 on the verge of the calamity of World War II has since been set to a number of tunes (most notably the haunting, yearning melody of *Llandaff*) and featured in a wide range of hymnals. That it appears usually amidst general rather than among Advent hymnody represents, perhaps, the need for re-imagining the season of Advent. At least that leads me to suggest it here as an apt summary of the answer to the informing question of this chapter, "What are we waiting for?"

> O Day of God draw nigh
> In beauty and in power,
> Come with thy timeless judgment now
> To match our present hour.
>
> Bring to our troubled minds,
> Uncertain and afraid,
> The quiet of a steadfast faith
> Calm of a call obeyed.
>
> Bring justice to our land,
> That all may dwell secure,
> And finely build for days to come
> Foundations that endure.
>
> Bring to our world of strife
> Thy sov'reign word of peace,
> That war may haunt the earth no more
> And desolation cease.

---

57. R.B.Y. Scott, a pastor in the Reformed tradition, became an Old Testament scholar and a professor successively at Union in Vancouver, British Columbia; McGill in Montreal, Quebec; and Princeton University, New Jersey. He contributed the poem to the Fellowship for a Christian Social Order. Cf., my commentary on the hymn in *The Hymnal 1982 Commentary*, vol. 3B, hymn 600/601 and biographical note in, vol. 2, 608–609 (New York: Church Publishing, 1994).

O Day of God draw nigh
As at creation's birth,
Let there be light again, and set
Thy judgments in the earth.[58]

In the present chapter we have also entertained the two conditions that will serve to instill such an eschatological imagination as is represented by this poem/hymn. The first, of course, rests on participatory worship that is well done. The second, more subtle consideration, is how such liturgy can, over time, actually be formative not only personally for the worshiper, but even more importantly, for the entire eucharistic assembly as a particular exhibition of the Body of Christ. It has already been noticed that the four weeks allotted to Advent are in themselves not adequate to the task. Hence, part of the double entendre, of our question "What are we waiting for?" is to suggest a season of sufficient length to meet the need. It has already been established that the lectionary itself is capable of bearing that load.

What has yet to be addressed are the considerable cultural obstacles to the re-imagination of Advent that is being proposed. These come in two sometimes interrelated forms, namely, the long custom for most of Western Christianity of observing a truncated season and, more seriously, the explicit competition and pernicious influence that is represented by the ubiquitous Christmas Culture of the contemporary world. All of that leads to the second question of this inquiry in the next chapter, "Why do we need to re-imagine Advent?"

---

58. The text of R.B.Y. Scott's poem is © Emmanuel College of Victoria University in the University of Toronto. Permission from Emmanuel College to cite the poem is gratefully acknowledged.

CHAPTER 2

Problems

Why Do We Need to Re-Imagine Advent?

Christianity long ago lost Advent to the global Christmas Culture. This is a fact in two ways. First, in general terms the season of Advent has been eclipsed by the pervasive commercialized and secularized anticipatory celebration of Christmas that begins months before December 25.[1] If Advent is recognized at all in such a world, it is co-opted as a late-coming, but welcomed occasion to give that Christmas Culture a further but now chocolate-coated countdown opportunity.[2] Second, Advent is, practically speaking, lost to the church when it yields to the temptations of complicity with this powerful and pervasive culture.

Taken together these two facts might in themselves provide reason enough for the church to re-imagine the season of Advent. Add to that what has been discovered in the discussion of Chapter 1 relative to the actual nature and

---

1. For the past decade I have kept annual files of notes and items clipped from publications and labeled "Advent Atrocities." These files have grown to include Christmas Culture references as well. For instance, I watch for the first indications of early Christmas advertisements in a range of media. What once appalled me as I caught a television Christmas ad on July 25, was demoted recently by one appearing in late June. There will be more from these files as this chapter develops. Suffice it for now to add that this does not even touch upon the existence of year-round boutiques totally devoted to the trappings of Christmas in towns and cities of any size.

2. Reference is made here, of course, to ubiquitous so-called (because now there are secular versions) Advent calendars that reward the daily count-downer with a piece of chocolate. (I say this even as one who heartily agrees with the message I once received on a birthday card: The outside proclaimed, "Chocolate is the answer!" and when opened, "The question is pretty much irrelevant.")

purpose of Advent and a "perfect storm" is created. In short, we may begin to suspect that the re-imagination of Advent might in fact be involved with the re-appropriation, proclamation, and exercise by the church of the Gospel's counter-cultural message. In any case, whether and to what degree such a re-imagination might be called for is the burden of this chapter. So, in the order indicated, attention is given first to the Advent that has been lost, second to the pervasiveness and power of the Christmas Culture, and lastly to several examples of the church's complicity with that culture. Chapter 3 then presents a re-imagined Advent in the face of such circumstances.

The Lost Advent

The season we have lost over the course of the last half-century did not appear all at once, neither did it come from a common venue, nor exhibit a singular emphasis. The Advent that we have known until recently gradually appeared over the course of several centuries. Although we have noted already the Orthodox exception to Advent being regarded as the beginning of the liturgical year, the first mention of something like an Advent season in the Western church comes in late-fifteenth century from northern Europe, specifically in a letter of the bishop of Tours in Gaul.[3] He mandates a lengthy period of fasting prior to the Christmas-Epiphany celebrations. If that ascetical strain provides the warp in the tapestry that came to be Advent, the woof was provided by the church in Rome. There, until the reforms generally grouped under the name "Gregorian" in recognition of their initiator, the new liturgical year had traditionally begun with the Vigil of Christmas and without such a preparatory season.[4] Whatever may have characterized it, that prior time appears to have been, rather, a year-end observance. The process of defining a four-week Advent, giving it an eschatological character,

---

3. Paul F. Bradshaw and Maxwell E. Johnson, *The Origins of Feasts, Fasts and Seasons in Early Christianity* (Collegeville, MN: Liturgical Press, 2011), 163. The authors note that Bp. Perpetuus, successor to St Martin of Tours, legislated a period of seven weeks of fasting from St. Martin's Day (November 11) to Christmas, but that (164) it is not until a century later that there is hard evidence of a "strongly ascetical" forty-day Advent season parallel to a pre-paschal Lent (Gregory of Tours, *History of the Franks*).

4. Pope St. Gregory the Great (*ca* 540–604) whose pontificate was from 590 until his death. He was known for his reforms, for voluminous pastoral correspondence and administrative expertise, and for missionary zeal (for example, sending Augustine of Canterbury to convert the English), all motivated by a vivid sense of the near end of things.

and establishing the season as the commencement of the liturgical year for the church in Rome, however, took the better part of the century after Gregory's pontificate.[5]

As the church in Rome became increasingly involved with the growing hegemony of the Frankish Empire in northern Europe, culminating in the papal crowning of Charlemagne as Holy Roman Emperor on Christmas Day in 800, there inevitably came to be a re-weaving of certain elements of the emerging tapestry of Advent. One result of this was the gradual, but hardly universal, adoption of the Roman pattern of a four-week Advent. But it also seems to be the case after the eighth century that the ascetical, penitential elements of the longer season of northern Europe exercised their influence on the piety of the shorter Advent period of Rome. Thus:

> What will happen is that the Roman Advent will eventually become imported elsewhere into Western Christianity, ultimately replacing the various local traditions, although Ambrosian and Mozarabic Rites will retain, even today, their customary six-week practice. And Advent itself will become in time a mixture of the various biblical, ascetic and eschatological orientations we have noticed.[6]

Even after the sixteenth-century Council of Trent when, in the face of the Protestant Reformations, the Roman Rite was declared as universal for that church, exceptions were allowed on the basis that certain rites could sustain their antiquity vis-à-vis the Roman liturgy. Particularly, as noted, this was so of the Mozarabic rite in Spain and the Ambrosian in Milan. Still today, for instance, the province of Milan observes a longer six-week Advent.

---

5. James McKinnon, *The Advent Project: The Later-Seventh Century Creation of the Roman Mass Proper* (Berkeley: University of California Press, 2000), especially the sections titled "Advent: Its Early History," "Calendric Versus Festal Church Year," and "Advent: The Chant Books," 146–153. McKinnon in the course of his massive study sets forth the Lateran's *schola cantorum*, established mid-seventh century, as the effective creator of the four-week Advent by the eighth century in Rome. Note: the similarity of name between the half-title of McKinnon's posthumously published work and The Advent Project Seminar of the NAAL is purely serendipitous.

6. Bradshaw and Johnson, *op cit*, 166. In their excellent sorting out of Advent, these scholars discuss the pros and cons of Advent's principal orientation—end of year? beginning of year? relation to Christmas?—as set forth by other leading liturgical theologians. In the end, however, they open a door to the proposal of the present book: "Of course, if Christmas itself is perceived not as the celebration of Jesus's nativity *in illo tempore*, that is, as a commemoration of a historical event or as Baby Jesus's birthday, but as itself a celebration of his *parousia*, his Advent, his coming again in glory, then an eschatologically oriented Advent season makes perfect sense." (168)

With respect to the influence of the ascetical piety of the longer period, however, the high- to late-medieval period witnessed a further and apocalyptic nuancing of Advent. In the face of terrifying events from the Viking incursions of the early Middle Ages to the devastating appearance of the Black Death in the fourteenth century, the medieval apocalyptic imagination added to the penitential and ascetic elements of the Advent mix yet another and persistent influence. Thereby, as liturgical theologian Patrick Malloy observes in discussing the development of the season, "the penitential and fearsome tenor of Advent was intensified."[7]

This brief unpacking of the Advent's complex origins and development has, if nothing else, revealed it to be something of an admixture and, in the event, not all that positive. Though the ascetical aspects of the season practically disappeared over the course of the latter half of the twentieth century, relief at the end of its rigors has been annually welcomed since at least the fifteenth century. That yearly end of Advent's ascetical aspect was popularly acknowledged in a poem/ditty—torn between relief and disdain!—for the last Sunday of the season:

Let Advent go, say all and some, say all and some!
Let Advent go, let Christmas come!

Yra, yra, y-sing, fa la la la la! Come jolly be, this Yuletide here!
Now once a year cast care aside and sing Fa la la la la!

We ate no meat, we ate no souse,* not meat nor souse,
But stinking fish not worth a louse! [*Refrain*]

The day of Christes feast natal, his feast natal,
We will be merry great and small. [*Refrain*]

And Advent now, O be thou shent,** O be thou shent!
It is enough to fast in Lent! [*Refrain*]   (*sausage; **shunned)[8]

---

7. Patrick Malloy, *Celebrating the Eucharist: A Practical Ceremonial Guide for Clergy and Other Liturgical Ministers* (New York: Church Publishing, 2007), 75.

8. Cited here with her permission, these verses are adapted by Pamela Grenfell Smith (www.baba-yaga.org) from a long sarcastic poem "Farewell to Advent" by James Ryman (*fl. c.* 1492) appearing in *The Oxford Book of Medieval English Verse,* edited by Celia and Kenneth Sisam, (Oxford: Clarendon Press, 1970), 504–506

The actual end of Advent's ascetical aspect is still, anachronistically, celebrated by some congregations through use of this text set to music after the dismissal on the last Sunday of Advent. In other words, the end of a penitentially constructed Advent which it celebrates has already long disappeared.

At least in form, the season itself, however, persists. Its character has already to some degree been re-imagined through the liturgical renewals reflected in the lectionaries. Whether that renewal has, practically speaking, been fully received by the church is another matter. Father Paul De Clerck, former director of the Institut Supérieur de Liturgie in l'Institut catholique de Paris, has doubts:

> Take the example of the Lectionary. Clearly it has been much enriched in comparison with what the old Roman Missal offered . . . But how has the proclamation of these pages of Scripture transformed the spirituality of the participants, whether they be priests or laypeople? Do these passages nourish the gospel life of the faithful who hear them? Do they recharge their spiritual batteries? I suspect not.[9]

Although a Roman Catholic context is addressed, the same reservations apply not only with regard to traditions making fulsome use of the *Revised Common Lectionary*, for example Anglican and Lutheran, but also in those churches that choose only one of the possible Scripture readings for Sundays.[10] In the face of this general non-reception our next concern will be to ask, "What forces militate against such reception, giving further cause, specifically, to re-imagine Advent?" This, of course, will involve some presentation and analysis of a fact of which everyone is eminently aware.

The Power of the Christmas Culture

In *Desiring the Kingdom*, the first volume of his in-depth study of world views and cultural formation, James K. A. Smith sets forth an anthropological

---

9. "The Liturgical Reform of Vatican II: Why Has It Only Been Partially Received?" in *Worship* (Collegeville, MN: Order of St. Benedict), March 2014, vol. 88.2, 171–172.

10. Many American Protestant churches, while using the *RCL*, employ a general order of worship rather than the classic four-fold Gather, Word, Table, Send, and, therefore, select only one Scripture reading (and possibly the indicated Psalm) from among the First, Epistle, and Gospel readings appointed for any particular Sunday.

analysis of human beings as primarily *desiring* creatures and only second-arily, that is, reflectively, as the *thinking* creatures we have complimented ourselves as being by the name *homo sapiens*. To be sure, the intellectual aspect of human being is of vital importance—we should not know our-selves to be primarily *desiring* creatures without the ability to take in the fact, as it were, and reflect upon both it and the choices we are led to make for good or ill.[11] He suggests on the basis of this analysis that human beings might better be described as *homo liturgicus*, that is, as worshiping creatures. This, of course, picks up on the synonymnity between worth (value) and worship. As such creatures we are susceptible to the power of persuasion to desire certain things or ends and, moreover, to find in them comprehensive solutions to our dis-ease, dysfunction, or disunity (the list could go on).

What we find of value or worth then, or perhaps what finds us, in the face of such dread or awe, we worship. That worship displays attitudes of trust and awe, or even performance of overt or covert ritual (liturgical) acts sig-nifying commitment to the object of our desires. Much of *Desiring the King-dom: Worship, Worldview, and Cultural Formation* is given to the presentation and analysis of powerful attractions for us toward such ends by, for instance, "consuming transcendence" (worship at the mall); "sacrificial violence" (the military-sports-entertainment complex), and "cathedrals of learning" (litur-gies and idolatries of the university). All of these compete powerfully for our attention and allegiance. But with regard to the present subject, it is the "consuming transcendence" or worship at the mall that relates directly to the power of the Christmas Culture.

Economically, Black Friday and Cyber Monday, those critical days fol-lowing Thanksgiving, often carry retail business into profitability for the year. And that means Christmas, at least commercially. This fact also accounts for the already noted ever-increasing push backward into the preceding months to mark the beginning of the season. From late August, Christmas decora-tions lurking in the back corners of mall stores, home supply chains, com-prehensive pharmacies, supermarkets, and specialty boutiques await the intervening celebration of Hallowe'en to pass. Overnight, by the morning

---

11. This is a summation of Smith's analysis which is treated at greater length in my review of his book in the *Anglican Theological Review*, vol. 94:4, 772–775.

of November 1, those back corner shelves and tables of all the aforementioned establishments have been completely transformed by a veritable explosion of Christmas decor throughout those venues—accompanied in most cases by endlessly supporting seasonal music. To complete this *parousia* comes the omnipresent and unrelenting barrage of advertisements. This music and media emphasis will last just long enough to cover the mayhem of post-Christmas Day sales.

Beyond the national particularities of this annual occurrence, the Christmas Culture has taken on global proportions, not limited in other words to North America or even to a post-Christian, secularized Europe. This fact can be revealed to us in a number of ways. In my own case, travels in service of the ecumenical movement have taken me to places where the presence and power of the Christmas Culture are impressively displayed: Harare and Johannesburg in Africa, Sydney in Australia, Hong Kong and Shanghai in Asia, and Caracas and Saõ Paulo in South America. Although such a list reflects personal observation, one need not travel to be aware of the global expanse of the culture. For instance, a glance at the label on the box containing one's most elegant Christmas ornament will probably read "Made in China" (where one-tenth of 1 percent of the population is Christian); or, perhaps, one will see with passing amazement, pausing only long enough to clip for the files, a *USA Today* photo of some twenty or so joyous men and women of Tokyo dressed in outfits denoting the popularity of Santa Claus in Japan.

All of this may simply attest to the ubiquity of the Christmas Culture while leaving untouched any consideration of its omnivorous power to transform or enlist elements of Christian worship into its service. Here, then, it might be well to adduce a compelling example of the Christmas Culture's ability to do precisely that. Music, and particularly the music of Christmas hymns or Yuletide carols, has already been noticed as a prized component in support of Christmas Culture attraction. Earlier, in Chapter 1, a "thought experiment" with a seminary liturgics class was recounted. Now I should like to propose a more general one involving a wider audience that includes anyone acquainted with the hymn/carol "Joy to the World" as set to what has become its most familiar tune, *Antioch*.

The thought experiment is this: imagine yourself sometime in early December asking a random variety of proverbial "persons on the street" to identify the genre of the music in the first bars of the tune *Antioch* that you articulate to them using singing syllables rather than words. It will, of course, help if you also imagine a microphone in hand and a back-up camera-bearer as well. My guess is that if particular persons among that variety of those quizzed know the melody, they will identify it as a Christmas carol, or even in many cases respond by saying, "Oh, yeah, it's 'Joy to the World.'" The variety encountered might include folks young and old, of various ethnicities, even, perhaps, secularized "nones" or even people of religions other than Christian.

Not to put too fine a point on it, the result of such a thought experiment might seem rather pedestrian. Everyone knows "Joy to the World" is a Christmas carol. The problem (as by now might be suspected) is that it simply is *not*. First of all, the composer of the text, Isaac Watts (1674–1748) first published it in his 1719 *Psalms of David, Imitated in the Language of the New Testament*. His major contributions as a hymnographer are immense and he is responsible for moving his own Reformed tradition from previous limitations in hymnody to the words of Scripture alone, to metrical or even paraphrased texts (hence the title of 1719). Secondly, however, as a Presbyterian of his age, he never would have set himself the task of composing a Christmas carol. The long Puritan/Nonconformist tradition in England stood firmly against any observance of a liturgical year, and much more against the celebration of Christmas with its own long tradition of accompanying not-to-be-countenanced revelries.

Given this information, a second look at the text itself seems to be in order. In four brief verses, it is a paraphrase of the second half of the regnal Psalm 98 *Cantate Domino* that begins "Sing to the Lord a new song, for he has done marvelous things." Watts's paraphrase is based on the second half of Psalm 98, verses 4–9 as they joyfully welcome the prospect of the Lord's coming to judge the earth:

> Make a joyful noise unto the Lord, all the earth:
> make a loud
> noise, and sing praise.
> Sing unto the Lord with the harp;
> with the harp,
> and the voice of a psalm.
> With trumpets and sound of cornet make a joyful noise
> before the Lord the King.

Let the sea roar, and the fulness thereof;
the world and they that dwell therein.
Let the floods clap their hands;
let the hills be joyful
together before the Lord.
For he cometh to judge the earth:
with righteousness shall he
judge the world, and the peoples with equity.[12]

Parenthetically, this text represents a view very different indeed from, on one hand, the medieval pessimism about God's coming judgment, and, on the other hand, contemporary apocalyptic visions of which we are aware today. The joyful welcome of the event belies the mood and manifestation of either contrary, but it also and pointedly explains why Isaac Watts titled his paraphrase, "The Messiah's coming and Kingdom."[13] To the degree that this is a startling revelation, it may be well to follow Watts's clue and re-read the original text of his hymn with Advent rather than Christmas eyes:

Joy to the world! the Lord is come:
let earth receive her King;
let every heart prepare him room,
and heaven and nature sing.

Joy to the world! the Savior reigns;
let us our songs employ,
while fields and floods, rocks, hills and plains,
repeat the sounding joy.

No more let sins and sorrows grow,
nor thorns infest the ground;
he comes to make his blessings flow
far as the curse is found.

---

12. This is the text of the second part of Psalm 98 that would have been before Watts by the time he lived, that is, probably from the Authorized (KJV) Version—as it is here—rather than the Geneva Bible.

13. *The Companion to the Hymnal 1982*, vol. 3A (New York: Church Hymnal Corp., 1994), 192.

He rules the world with truth and grace,
and makes the nations prove
the glories of his righteousness,
and wonders of his love.[14]

Clearly, the venue envisioned is not a manger in Bethlehem, but the entire earth. Nor is the image one of infant hands improbably wielding a royal orb and scepter, but of a Sovereign Christ bringing the nations from the murderous curse of Cain to a state of peace and justice by proving "the wonders of his love." Watts has here purposely transformed the God of Psalm 98 into the Messiah of the Christian tradition. Beyond that, his paraphrase envisions the presence of the Reign of God / Kingdom of Christ in a world transformed from its "normal" warfare and violence into something more like the peaceable kingdom of Isaiah 65:17–25 or the vision of leaves from the tree of life being for the healing of the nations in Revelation 22:2, so that the seeds of Cain's thorn bush no longer infest the earth. But, of course, what most of us envision on the screen of our consciousness as we sing or hear these words to the tune *Antioch* is something quite different and probably more like a kind of crowned Infant of Prague reigning from the cradle—scarcely such an informing image to be entertained by a Calvinist such as Watts!

Oddly, this hymn had a difficult time making it into the Christmas section of the Episcopal Church's *Hymnal 1982* and thereby hangs a tale—briefly told—of the power in the Christmas Culture. By 1871 Watts's hymn, conjoined to Handel's triumphant tune *Antioch* (as adapted by American hymnographer Lowell Mason), had entered the hymnals of many traditions. In the Episcopal Church tradition, however, it continued to appear as late as *The Hymnal 1940* in the section of General Hymns conjoined solely to the less spectacular tune Richmond. As for the other traditions, the hymn sung to Antioch progressed along the arc of the developing Christmas Culture. The trajectory of that arc can be specifically traced from 1843 with the publication of Charles Dickens's *A Christmas Carol* and the ensuing mid-Victorian

---

14. *The Hymnal 1982* (New York: Church Hymnal Corp., 1985), hymn 100. Refrains were added later.

nostalgic observance of imagined Christmases past in the yearly celebration of Christmas present in both England and America—and, it may be added, with little presage of what enormities might appear from the advent of the spirit of Christmas yet-to-come in a secularized world.[15]

It was not until *The Hymnal 1982* that the Episcopal Church capitulated to internal popular pressures and included "Joy to the World" set to *Antioch* and placed it prominently as hymn 100 in the section of Christmas Season hymns. All of this, it must be said, is adduced for the sole purpose of demonstrating through one starkly clear example the power that the Christmas Culture has to enlist elements—in this case musical—of a prior ecclesial culture but now in service of its own ends. And in this case, the co-option is made more egregious by presenting and employing something exactly contrary to its origin in Scripture and its author's intention. In short, what is clearly about the full and final manifestation of the Reign of God / Kingdom of Christ is put forth as a carol principally referencing the birth of Jesus. The subversion is complete and the power of the Christmas Culture manifest.

In his pioneering study *The Origins of the Liturgical Year*, Thomas J. Talley rather laconically explained the admixtures of the Advent season by remarking, "In ritual cycles, the beginning and end times meet, and the liturgical year is no exception."[16] He suggests, perhaps, a blending of images in the alternating current that is imagined in such meetings. But with the intervention of the powerful Christmas Culture it also appears that some sorting out of the connections might be in order precisely to avoid the short-circuiting of the seasons themselves. In any case, it is to such a sorting out that this discussion now turns as the temptation is presented to the church to fall into complicity with a contravening and demonstrably powerful Christmas Culture. The result of such a complicity may, in fact, compromise the integrity of one or the other, or what is more likely, both, the Advent and the Christmas-to-Epiphany season.

---

15. The discussion of this paragraph in its factual details concerning the poem and its tunes is based on the commentary found in *The Companion to the Hymnal 1982*, vol. 3A (New York: Church Hymnal Corp., 1994), 192–197. On a personal note, I can attest to the fact that as a cathedral boy chorister and then choir member in the late 1940s and through the 1950s we never once sang this hymn at Christmastide. That was a puzzlement, even then.

16. Thomas J. Talley, *The Origins of the Liturgical Year*, 2nd ed. (Collegeville, MN: Liturgical Press, 1986), 80.

The Church's Complicity with the Culture

It is ironic that within the previously mentioned "Advent Atrocities" files kept by me for over a decade, the most glaring example of ecclesial complicity with the Christmas Culture should have occurred on my own threshold, as it were. It involves an announcement published in our regional newspaper and comes from a congregation of a tradition not my own, but in my own township. Here it is for Advent 1, 2013:

> On Sunday there will be an Advent pancake breakfast between the 8 and 10 a.m. services at Church of the [redacted]. Children are especially invited to come and meet Santa Claus and the Baby Jesus.[17]

And here also one encounters two atrocities for the price of one, to say nothing of the date itself: the juxtaposition of "Advent" and "Santa Claus" stand out at first, but, secondly, note well the order of importance in the formational invitation extended to the children: first Santa and then the Baby Jesus! This situation could only be redeemed by reference to the amazingly anachronistic and pure-kitsch porcelain knicknack, seasonally advertised, of Santa Claus, tasseled cap in hand, kneeling at Jesus's *crèche* . . . (seeking forgiveness?).

One is torn between the hope that this is a singular occurrence and the suspicion that, given the ubiquity and influence of the Christmas Culture, similar occurrences of that atrocity have happened or will happen elsewhere in ecclesial settings. But this is perhaps too crass an example to really plumb the depths of the church's complicity with the culture. It is more often the case that subtler incursions are made. Take, for instance, the tradition—once purely Anglican, but now widely ecumenical—of a Service of Lessons and Carols. Somewhat paralleling the Great Vigil of Easter, it was set forth in the early twentieth century and quickly became established in the Church of England. From there it came to North America and other parts of the Anglican world and, finally, into other traditions. Though this service was intended originally for Christmas Eve, in today's Christmas Culture one finds all-too-often a Christmas Lessons and Carols service featured in many congrega-

---

17. "Church Services," *Democrat & Chronicle* (Rochester, NY: Gannett Publishers, 2013). I have left out the name of the congregation to protect both it and the denomination involved.

tions of various traditions on what is presently the first Sunday of Advent in late November or early December.[18] In addition, the more recent creation of early-season services generally called "Advent Lessons and Carols" have appeared in an attempt to mitigate the incongruity. In the end, however, these services frequently rest upon the same base: a pilgrimage through Scripture and song to Bethlehem, rather than a hopeful celebration of the *eschaton* we await in the full manifestation of the Reign of God / Kingdom of Christ.

A third and more comprehensive example of the complicity under investigation might provide a more convincing capstone example of why we might need to re-imagine the Advent season. And, in this regard, it will be well to draw from my own tradition so as to avoid any charge of casting aspersions upon others. Furthermore, it will be important to disguise the actual congregation and for this, my particular circumstances prove useful. As indicated earlier, extensive travels on ecumenical or other church business have often taken me far afield from the hometown parish where my family are members.

On the first Sunday of a four-week Advent in a recent year, I had occasion to be an observer-participant in the regular choral Eucharist of a congregation of the Episcopal Church, beginning at 10:00 a.m. It is from that experience that the following description and commentary are drawn in illustration of the fact of the church's complicity with the Christmas Culture. The argument here will rest, therefore, on a kind of *ex uno disce omnes* basis, that is, from one example the whole situation may be discerned. In other words, my conclusion will be, again, that this one instance in a particular tradition will not be exceptional and that, with allowances made for variations in denominational context or worship *ordo*, something very similar can and does occur elsewhere. The pattern of worship for the example given here is the normal four-fold one of Gathering, Word, Table, Sending.

Gathering Rite. After a promising opening with the processional hymn "Come, Thou Long Expected Jesus" the liturgy featured two Gathering Rites. The first of these involved a family of the congregation coming forward from

---

18. The service was originally compiled by Edward Benson, then bishop of Truro (Cornwall) and later (1883–1896) archbishop of Canterbury. "A Service of Nine Lessons and Carols" was first observed at the Truro cathedral on Christmas Eve 1880. Its present and most famous exhibition, as modified by Eric Milner-White in 1918, comes annually on Christmas Eve from King's College, Cambridge, and is broadcast globally by BBC.

the nave and gathering around the Advent wreath in the sanctuary. After a brief dialogue between the younger child of the family and the congregation the first candle on the wreath was lighted. The dialogue indicated that this light was the beginning of what would be an illuminated path to Bethlehem over the next weeks.[19] In effect, then, the assembly had been gathered for worship at the beginning of a new season. At this point, however, the rector began the liturgy again with the standard (and very appropriate to Advent) doxological greeting to the congregation, "Blessed be God" to which came the regular response, "And blessed be God's Kingdom, now and forever." This was followed by the Collect for Purity, the singing of the *Kyrie eleison* (probably not in deference to an earlier penitential construction of Advent, but because it takes less time than the *Gloria in excelsis*, thus conceding that the first Gathering Rite had consumed some minutes). This second Gathering Rite was then concluded with the thematic Sunday collect set for the beginning of the season. This prayer, originally composed by Cranmer for the 1549 Book of Common Prayer, alludes to Paul's admonition to us in Romans 13—a call to cast away the works of darkness and put on the "armor of light" now (as the prayer continues):

> in the time of this mortal life in which your Son Jesus Christ came to visit us in great humility; that in the last day, when he shall come again in his glorious majesty to judge both the living and the dead, we may rise to the life immortal; through him who lives and reigns with you and the Holy Spirit, one God, now and for ever. *Amen.*[20]

So, being twice-gathered with somewhat bifurcated understandings of the season's principal focus we limped on to the next portion of the liturgy, which (I hoped) might help to clarify the apparent confusion.

Word. Alas, it was not to be so. To be sure the first two lections and psalm, appropriately led by members of the congregation trained as lectors, set before us readings for Year A with clear Advent themes: from Isaiah 2:1–5 we looked forward to a time when nations would not learn war anymore;

---

19. Questions surrounding the Advent wreath and the para-liturgies that have grown up around it as well as what such a wreath would look like in an expanded Advent season will be addressed in Chapter 5. For the present it is sufficient to note the fact of these para-liturgies and the false step taken.

20. Book of Common Prayer (1979), 211.

in unison with Psalm 122 we prayed urgently "for the peace of Jerusalem" (lamentably still necessary); and then from Paul again in Romans 13:11–14 we learned more urgently that the night is nearly over and salvation at hand. Next with the singing of "I Want to Walk as a Child of the Light," the Gospel book was processed into the midst of the assembly and the priest proclaimed from Matthew 24:36–44, again urgently, that we should be alert and pay attention since the Son of Man is coming at an unexpected moment. With such readings upon which to draw, I expected the homily to usher us truly into the implications of the season's keen anticipation as set forth by the proclamation of Scripture. Instead, however, the collect and lections, including the Gospel, were totally ignored by the preacher in favor of a sermon that explored the four weeks of Advent as a time of preparation for the Nativity on Christmas Eve. Now, in a reminiscent mood of dark despair, I cannot remember the Prayers of the People chosen to form our response to God's word and the antithetical musings of the rector's homily.[21]

Table. With the announcement of the offertory, I briefly entertained the hope that the first Sunday of Advent might yet be salvaged. During the preparation of the oblations of bread and wine on the altar and the collection of the people's offerings, we were, however, treated by the choir to an anthem titled ... (wait for it) ... "*Mary Had A Baby.*" Evidently, the church musician had also perfectly prepared for a premature Nativity. And for the first time in my life I entertained the possibility of walking out before communion and taking an earlier flight for home. In the event, I did not. The rector's and choir's previous thoughts and song to the contrary notwithstanding, a great theme of Advent now came before us in the Proper Preface of the Eucharistic Prayer, establishing that we give thanks:

> Because you sent your beloved Son to redeem us from sin and death, and to make us heirs in him of everlasting life; that when he shall come again in power and great triumph to judge the world, we may without *shame* or *fear* rejoice to behold his appearing... [to the *Sanctus*][22]

---

21. Lutherans have a wonderful tradition that I wish Episcopalians would adopt, namely, singing a "Hymn of the Day" just after the sermon. Somewhat perversely for a cleric, I have always regarded this custom as redemptive. For no matter how dreadful the homily (and I would include some of my own in the count), the situation can still be saved by the congregation's robust singing of a tried and tested text and tune.

22. Book of Common Prayer (1979), 378. Emphases added.

Shame at this liturgical travesty in my own tradition was certainly an emotion that I was experiencing and, to be honest, a bit of fear that if the *parousia* should occur at the moment, we would all be doomed. Yet music once again redeemed my fears and saved the day as we sang for the communion hymn "Let All Mortal Flesh Keep Silence." This, I prayed, in regard to the present liturgy, was a consummation devoutly to be desired!

Sending. But the nightmare was not yet over. In that particular congregation, parish announcements follow the usual post-communion sending prayer and blessing. The option of a blessing specific to Advent from several provided in the *Book of Occasional Services* was not exercised—possibly because they stand rather over against the practical tenor of that particular liturgy. These announcements, nevertheless, brought verbally to our attention matters noted in print at the back of the service bulletin. Particularly emphasized were two: first, that the normal readings for the liturgy of the word on the second Sunday of Advent next week would not be used, but rather, a service of Lessons and Carols (with special music from the choir) would occur in their place; and second, that there would be no sermon on the third Sunday of Advent in favor of devoting that block of time to the children's presentation of a Nativity pageant (since the fourth Sunday of Advent fell too close to Christmas that year to ensure a full cast due to family holiday travels). When we were finally dismissed with "Let us bless the Lord," my responding "Thanks be to God" was perhaps uttered more emphatically than is usual. Gratefully, for the remainder of that Advent, I would be worshiping elsewhere.

Summation and Transition

All of us who teach seminarians the principles of worship according to a matrix of best practices have over the years collected a repertoire of real-life examples that frankly comprise a catalogue of liturgical horror stories. At appropriate junctures, we tell these in class with the tacit or explicit intention of saying to those given to us for formation, "Don't do that!" And, of course, we also tell these stories among ourselves, making light (like Hobbits) of matters very serious to us and, indeed, to the whole church. This recounting of an actual Advent worship experience fulfills both of the teaching and collegial functions as noted, but here it is also in service to the focus of this chapter, namely, to indicate why we might need to re-imagine Advent. Obviously, from the implied or explicit contrasting of what might have been on that particular Sunday, there is much within the Scripture and tradition that is significantly counter-cultural in the best sense of the phrase. And, indeed, these things have vital connection to the church's life and mission. The Christmas Culture will go on its "merry" way for the foreseeable future. There is every reason, nevertheless, for Christians to offer and live out a different and counter-cultural alternative, inspired by a worship congruent with the principal focus of the season.

Three areas in this chapter, then, have provided points of focus for the need to re-imagine Advent. First, the rather late and mixed origins of Advent were explored along with some re-imaginings over time of the nature and focus of the season. Second, the pervasive and pernicious influence and power of the relatively new fact of a global Christmas Culture have been investigated. That discussion revealed aspects inimical to or distorting of authentic Advent themes and the integrity of the season itself, whether construed in a shorter or longer period. And finally, three examples of the church's yielding to complicity with that Christmas Culture were adduced and explored with the implication that a longer season than the present four weeks of Advent might be part of the remedy, the more so as the truncated version stands no chance against the surrounding culture.

The presentations of Chapter 1, "Expectations," regarding the intended nature and purpose of Advent as rooted in the lectionaries, conjoined to the reflections of the present chapter concerned with "Problems," combine, then, to give ample cause for the need to re-imagine Advent not only presently, but for time to come. It will be the business of the next chapter, "Solutions," drawing upon resources in the long tradition as well as meeting contemporary challenges, to address what might be the shape and feel of such a re-imagined Advent. From that perspective Chapters 4 and 5 will, respectively, present pertinent resources and attend to practical pastoral concerns in implementing such resources for the life and mission of the church.

CHAPTER 3

Solutions

What Would Be the Shape and Feel of Such an Advent?

The proposal for an expanded Advent, as we have seen in the first chapter, is rooted in a simple idea: to render the Advent we keep congruent with the lectionary we have. To this only was added, "everything else is commentary." Thus in the second chapter the commentary began by exploring the stark contrast between the central focus of our thematic scriptural readings for the season and the surrounding global Christmas Culture. We noted how that culture, vestigially rooted in Christian themes, could and, in fact, does subvert the principal focus of Advent. Now the task of commentary turns more positively to setting forth the dimensions and character of an expanded season, in other words, what would be the shape and feel of such an Advent?

Calendar

The calendar of the ecclesial year was one of the important subjects of the liturgical reforms initiated by the Roman Catholic Church's Second Vatican Council and all traditions using the Western liturgical year were subsequently, some even concomitantly, affected by that renewal. One of the principal features of the reform was the declaration that each and every Sunday of the entire year would be designated and serve as a feast of Christ.[1] This

---

1. Constitution on the Sacred Liturgy, esp. ¶ 106, 169, *The Documents of Vatican II*. Walter M. Abbott, SJ, ed. (New York: The America Press, 1966). For the Roman Catholic Church this decree precluded the intrusion upon Sundays of the *sanctorale* (commemoration of saints). Anglicans,

determination placed renewed emphasis on the Sunday liturgy as celebrating the entire Paschal mystery: the passion, death, resurrection, ascension of Jesus Christ, including the sending of the Holy Spirit.

Even as the Sunday worship is, then, to be focused in this way, the Constitution on the Sacred Liturgy also sets forth the formational importance of Scripture as providing the thematic focus of any given Sunday.[2] It has already been noted in the second chapter that in the calendar revision that followed upon Vatican II, consideration was given to a significant lengthening of Advent as over against proposals to give the short season a totally incarnational focus compliant with the global Christmas Culture emerging after World War II. The compromise reached retained the truncated season, but ensured an all-but-total eschatological emphasis. In this regard, the scriptural content of that compromise should not be missed. The last weeks of the liturgical year and the first weeks of the new in the lectionary were accorded lections focused on eschatology, or, as we have been calling it, "the full manifestation of the Reign of God / Kingdom of Christ." In the spirit of Vatican II, this decision flowed into the ecumenical project of a common lectionary for all traditions. So today, whether the *Ordo Lectionum Missae* (*OLM*) of the Roman Church or the *Revised Common Lectionary* (*RCL*) of the other churches is in use, the emphasis for an expanded Advent is the same.[3]

If what has been said thus far gives some basic substance to the content of an expanded Advent, it now becomes essential to discern what would be the basic structure or pattern of the season. In an expanded Advent, the earliest

---

Lutherans, and other Protestants observing the liturgical calendar were encouraged in this regard to keep the seasonal focus on the Lord's Day in contrast to the multiplication of Sundays particularly devoted to worthwhile but potentially distracting emphases or causes.

2. "Constitution on the Sacred Liturgy," *Documents of Vatican II*, ¶ 24, 147.

3. The online Appendices of this book compare the *OLM* and *RCL* lections for the seven weeks of an expanded Advent. In these I have provided a capsule statement of the central theme of each of the sixty-three possible readings in the three-year cycle of readings for both lectionaries. A close examination of these *préces* will disclose the overwhelming eschatological focus of the weeks, except the last, which begins the transition to an incarnational emphasis. Between the *OLM* and the *RCL* only three of twenty-one possible Gospel readings differ (and where they do, they are simply from different parts of the same Gospel's chapter or section and thus congruent in theme). Of the twenty-one possible Epistle readings, only two differ but the congruency persists. Nearly half (ten of twenty-one) of the Old Testament readings, however, are different. All but one of these occur in the three-year cycle during the first four weeks of an expanded Advent, but, once again, though the readings differ between *OLM* and *RCL*, a comparison of the *préces* shows congruent focus. Cf. www.churchpublishing.org/whatarewewaitingfor.

date upon which Advent 1 would occur is November 5 and the latest date would be November 12. The ordering works out thus:

Advent 1	*the Sunday falling on or between*	November 5–12
Advent 2	*the Sunday falling on or between*	November 13–19
Advent 3	*the Sunday falling on or between*	November 20–26
Advent 4	*the Sunday falling on or between*	November 27–Dec. 7
Advent 5	*the Sunday falling on or between*	December 4–10
Advent 6	*the Sunday falling on or between*	December 11–17
Advent 7	*the Sunday falling on or between*	December 18–24

Two questions might immediately come to mind in regard to this dating. First, and more general in ecumenical scope, would Advent 3 displace the Feast of Christ the King (or Reign of Christ)? This designation has been on the Roman Catholic calendar since 1925 (though only on its present date since 1969) and in the last third of the twentieth entury has been accorded ecumenical reception by traditions following a liturgical calendar. The second question, more specific to Anglicans, has to do with what happens when Advent 1 and All Saints' Sunday coincide. This potential conflict arises occasionally in those years when the Sunday following November 1 falls on the fifth through the seventh (that is, the observance of All Saints' Sunday). Alternative possibilities for resolving this conflict are addressed in our fifth chapter "Concerns," since the issue generally affects only one tradition. The wider and ecumenical question as to whether Christ the King (Reign of Christ) Sunday is eclipsed by Advent 3 in an expanded season forms a pivotal part of the season's substance. And it is to that discussion that we now turn.

Content

As already established according to the new or renewed rubric, every Sunday must be a feast of Christ. But for the Sundays of an expanded Advent we can also look to something old, in the sense of venerable, if not ancient. Like a "scribe trained for the kingdom of heaven" (Matt. 13:52) we thus bring out

of the treasure house of Scripture and tradition something old and something new, or, rather, we can take something long-revered and apply it anew.
The reference here is to the seven Great "O" Antiphons.

Everyone who knows these antiphons in their original placement cher-
ishes them. But beyond that, it would be difficult to find a Christian who does
not know them. Audacious as that claim may initially appear, this is the case
simply because most know the Great "O" Antiphons as they appear in their
compacted form as the verses of the familiar Advent hymn "O Come, O Come
Emmanuel." In order to certify the propriety of these texts before applying
them in the present situation, it will be well to rehearse their pedigree.

Since later than the eighth entury and possibly even earlier in the Western church,[4] the women and men of monastic communities sang these Great
"O" Antiphons as appropriate framing for the canticle taken from Luke's
Gospel and known as the *Magnificat* (Song of Mary).[5] The texts get their
name from the inclusion of an "O" of address before each of the titles for
the Messiah or Christ that the monastics gleaned from their constant attention to Scripture throughout the cycle of the year in the daily prayer offices
of their communities. And it was from the seventeenth through the twen-
ty-third of December that they sang the "O" antiphons, which take their
names from the first word or words of these titles from the Bible:

O Sapientia	(Wisdom)	Sir. 24:3, Wis. 8:1[6]
O Adonai	(Lord)	Exod. 3:2–6, Isa. 6:3, 1 Cor. 2:8

---

4. *Oxford Dictionary of the Christian Church* (*ODCC*), 3rd ed. (New York: Oxford University
Press, 1997), 1169. On the basis of possible reference to them by Boethius (*c.* 480–*c.* 524), other
authorities date the appearance of these antiphons even earlier.

5. Luke 1:46–55 "My soul magnifies the Lord". . . " The evangelist includes this, of course, as
Mary's ode in response to the Annunciation by the archangel Gabriel, but also as the canticle lays
out with some specificity the values of the Kingdom that will be established with the birth of the
Messiah. The *Magnificat* continues to be the set canticle after the first reading at Evensong/Vespers
in the Daily Office.

6. These citations are not exhaustive, but only indicative. The apocryphal Wisdom books were
in the canon of scripture for all until the sixteenth-century reformations. After that, the books of the
Apocrypha were excluded from the Bible by most Protestants, but Anglicans retained reading of
them in the Daily Office and Eucharist for edification only and not to prove any point of doctrine
[cf. Article VI, Articles of Religion, Book of Common Prayer 1979 (New York: Church Publishing),
868.] If one wanted a New Testament *locus* to support the *Sapientia* Christ-title, it can be found,
for example, in 1 Cor. 1:24 ("Christ. . . the wisdom of God), or Christ in the *Logos* theology of the
Fourth Gospel.

O Radix Jesse	(Root of Jesse)	Isa. 11:10, Rom. 15:11–12
O Clavis David	(Key of David)	Isa. 22:22, Rev. 3:7
O Oriens	(Morning Star)	Isa. 60:3, Hos. 6:3, Mal. 4:2, Luke 1:7
O Rex gentium	(King of nations)	Ps. 99:1, 4; Rev. 11:15, 15:3
O Emmanuel	(God with us)	Isa. 7:4, 33:22, Matt. 1:23

Over time the singing of these antiphons was marked by the prolonged sonorous chanting of the intial "O" and various officers of the community (for example, abbot/abbess, precentor, prior, cellerar, and so on) were assigned particular antiphons. During the Middle Ages, the English even added an eighth antiphon for the day prior to Christmas Eve, thus bumping *O Sapientia* back to December 16.[7] But for the most part, the spirit of the age was more than content with the number seven as an organizing principle for many things. This was especially so as the clever sometimes arranged the antiphons in such a way that when the initial letters of the titles were read backward they formed the Latin phrase *Ero cras*, which translated is "I shall be present tomorrow" (that is, Christmas Eve).[8] This acrostic puzzle notwithstanding, there is a larger point to be discerned in such medieval playfulness: in a well-tuned Christian spirituality, forward or backward in time at any point, Christ is all-in-all.

Yet the eschatological affirmation of that larger point remained behind cloister doors until the seventeenth century when a creative venture in hymnography began to open these antiphons to a wider Christian audience. An unknown author composed verses on the antiphons emphasizing in particular their petitions and these were first published in *Psalteriolum Cantionum Catholicarum* (Cologne, 1710) and came into use by the

7. It was an antiphon designed to accord devotion to Mary, the one originally exclaiming the *Magnificat*; hence *O Virgo virginum*—"O Virgin of virgins." This survived even the turbulence of the sixteenth and seventeenth centuries: though the monastic communities had been dissolved for more than a century, the calendar in 1662 BCP continued to show December 16 instead of 17 as *O Sapientia*. Cf. BCP 1662 and *ODCC*, 1169 for the point.

8. Cf. Commentary on "O Come, O Come Emmanuel," hymn 56, *The Hymnal 1982 Companion*, vol. 3 A, Raymond E. Glover, ed. (New York: Church Publishing, 1994), 103. The *ero cras* arrangement was not, however, a universal practice with regard to the "O" antiphons. Cf. footnote 21 below.

mid-nineteenth century for English-speaking congregations through the translations of the great Anglican liturgist John Mason Neale.[9] In the event, this development condensed the Great "O" Antiphons by removing them from contextual association with the *Magnificat* on the last days of Advent. Their appearance as a hymn freed them to become a familiar song of the entire season. Furthermore, to change the image from an aural to a visual one, the development of the hymn "Veni, Veni Emmanuel" accompanied by its fifteenth-century plainsong tune enabled these scriptural titles of the Messiah to be displayed upon a much larger canvas throughout the church. If nothing else, the general reception of the hymn by a vast number of traditions attests to that fact.

The proposal for an expanded Advent in our own time seeks not only to respect the original statement and setting of the Great "O" Antiphons *as well as* their later hymn form, but to project them onto an even larger screen to meet the exigencies of our age and, in fact, the future as well. Part of the re-imagining of Advent discussed in the previous chapter is directly to apply the messianic titles of the antiphons to the seven Sundays of an expanded Advent. Brief commentary on how this may be done will conclude this chapter. Yet it is important to note here that using these Christ-titles to mark the Sundays of Advent observes and honors the rule that every Lord's Day of the liturgical year is a feast of Christ. And, in this case, the titles especially elucidate and emphasize the eschatological focus of the season precisely because they are drawn out of the covenants of ancient Scripture and look forward to the fullest manifestation of that promise. In the liturgy of Advent, we encounter the referenced Christ, not just as perceivers of the fact, but far more as participants in the process. And that participation is to be carried into the new year.

Character

At least three aspects in the process of setting out the character of these Sundays in an expanded Advent bear initial mention. First, a certain progression—indeed integral to the Great "O" Antiphons on any scale—can be immediately discerned. The progression begins with the widest possible, in

---

9. Cf. *The Hymnal 1982 Companion*, vol. 3A, 102–106 for a detailed account of this fascinating story.

fact cosmic, scope with the divine *Wisdom / Sapientia* creating and sustaining the unimaginably vast universe. And then, secondly, there is an onward movement through historical time that keeps before the People of God their rich heritage (having also the added benefit of constant reminder to Christians that we are guests within that fold). The penultimate link, specifically referencing Christ's resurrection, brings us to that threshold where we begin to acknowledge the cosmic contained and present within the particular of *Emmanuel / God with us.*

Perhaps the seventeenth-century Anglican poet John Donne caught this liminality best as he exclaimed in regard to the bearer of the eternal Word, "Thou hast light in darke; and shutst in little roome, *Immensity cloystered in thy deare wombe.*"[10] As we transition at the end point of this threshold season into the new liturgical year, the third (and eschatological) point of discernment is not to be abandoned in the event, but carried with us into the annual round of observance and celebration throughout the year. The Sunday placement of these seven titles of the Messiah or Christ gives to the worshiping assembly a present focus for the past and the future. Out of Scripture and long usage, each of these names calls to mind a crucial, not to say salvific, past event or disposition.

Each of the titles also evokes, perhaps it is not too strange to say *remembers*, the future as we look to fulfilment or full manifestation of the particular title.[11] Textually speaking, the premiere liturgical exhibition of this meeting point of time and eternity occurs with the congregation's acclamation in the midst of the Eucharistic Prayer or Great Thanksgiving. In contemporary liturgy it is variously expressed, but perhaps most frequently as "Christ has died, Christ is risen, Christ will come again." Here time past and time future are ecstatically collapsed into the evanescence of time present. The claim here is that as foci for the Sundays of an expanded Advent, each of these names for the Anointed One bears precisely such eschatological and formational weight. We turn then to the character of the specific Messianic titles.

---

10. Final couplet of the sonnet "Annunciation" in *La Corona*, circle of praise taking its coronal or circular structure from the round of the ecclesiastical year. *John Donne*, John Hayward, ed. (Baltimore: The Penguin Poets, 1960), 164. Emphasis in original.

11. See the discussion in the "Parousia" section of Chapter 1 on Emma O'Donnell, *Remembering the Future: The Experience of Time in Jewish and Christian Liturgy* (Collegeville, MN: Liturgical Press, 2015), and for the present point especially her Chapter 9: "The Liturgical Transformation of Time: Ritual, Repetition, and Flow."

Advent 1: Sapientia / Wisdom Sunday
(November 5–12)

This title of the Messiah or Christ is drawn from the Wisdom literature of the Bible. This genre is generally regarded as a third classification along with the Law and the Prophets in our common Judeo-Christian tradition. One of the remarkable aspects of the literature is the personification of Wisdom. Wisdom is seen as reaching back into the tradition to interpret for the present the meaning of past events. For instance, in the key experience of their liberation, the People of God are envisioned as singing this paean of praise:

> Wisdom freed from a nation of oppressors
> > a holy people and a blameless race;
> She entered the soul of a servant of the Lord,
> > withstood dread rulers with wonders and signs.
> To the saints she gave the reward of their labors,
> > and led them by a marvelous way;
> She was their shelter by day
> > and a blaze of stars by night.
> She brought them across the Red Sea,
> > she led them through mighty waters;
> But their enemies she swallowed in the waves
> > and spewed them out from the depths of the abyss.
> And then, Lord, the righteous sang hymns to your Name,
> > and praised with one voice your protecting hand;
> For Wisdom opened the mouths of the mute,
> > and gave speech to the tongues of a new-born people.[12]

Yet developments of this theme of Wisdom personified provide even greater scope. Wisdom is seen as the first of all, the one through whom the One Eternal God brings everything into existence and imbues creation with her gifts.[13] Such considerations led the Psalmist to exclaim, "O LORD, how manifold are your works! In wisdom you have made them all . . ." (Ps. 104:24).

---

12. Wisdom of Solomon 10:15–19, 20b–21. This translation is found in *Enriching Our Worship 1* (New York: Church Publishing, 1998), Canticle A, 30.

13. Wisdom of Jesus the Son of Sirach, *The Holy Bible: New Revised Standard Version* (NY:New York: Oxford University Press, 1989), chapter 24, verses 1–6 esp.

More pointedly, Wisdom is proclaimed as the first of the seven spiritual gifts that will characterize the Messianic King in the vision of Isaiah.[14] As further developed in the early Christian tradition this same creative Wisdom is identified with the divine Logos or Word that creates and sustains the cosmos.[15]

There is, then, in the Wisdom / *Sapientia* title for Christ a rich, not to say inexhaustible, focus for the observance of the first Sunday in an expanded Advent.

Advent 2: Adonai Sunday
(November 13–19)

It is more than interesting that the long tradition of the Great "O" Antiphons preserved for Christians the Jewish practice of voicing the word *Adonai* whenever the sacred four-letter YHWH name of God appeared in Scripture.[16] The word *Kyrie* (Lord) could easily have been employed as it was in the Greek translations of the Hebrew Scriptures. But that would scarcely have carried the weight of reference intended by the antiphon itself. For here the Eternal One is addressed not only as "Lord of all the earth,"[17] but as the leader of the house of Israel who, in the words of the hymn, "in ancient times didst give the Law in cloud and majesty and awe."[18]

With this Sunday, then, we move from the wider cosmic purview into a more specific focus. We are put in mind of our participatory heritage in and as the People of God. As such, our very constitution as a people with a mission in the world is vividly brought before us. The constituting Law, given by

---

14. Isaiah 11:2. These gifts are ingrafted into the Christian tradition as referring to Christ and, as such, these seven formational spiritual gifts (or divine energies) are received for life by all Christians at their full baptismal initiation into the Body of Christ.

15. As previously mentioned, this is especially to be found in the remarkable Prologue to the Fourth Gospel.

16. It was not until early English editions of the KJV Bible came into use that the erroneous word "Jehovah" appeared as the name of God. The mistake is often attributed to Peter Galatinus around 1520 as originally attempting to pronounce the sacred consonants of the divine name using the vowel pointings for the word "Adonai." These vowel pointings had been inserted into the text by the Masoretes. Cf. especially, the *Interpreter's Dictionary of the Bible* (Nashville: Abingdon Press, 1962), vol. 2, 817 "Jehovah" and vol. 3, 150 "Lord."

17. This occurs often in the Psalter, but specifically to the point in Ps. 97:5b, a central citation in a grouping of Psalms acclaiming the all-encompassing sovereignty of God.

18. The Latin text is emphatic on the point: *O Adonai, et Dux domus Israel, qui Moysi in igne flammae rubi apparuisti, et ei in Sina legem dedisti: veni ad redimendum nos in brachio extento*, literally, "O Lord, and Leader of the house of Israel, who appeared to Moses in flaming red fire, and in Sinai gave the law. . . . "

this *Adonai*, assumes that there is One who values us and whom we may—among many distracting alternatives—worship. This Law also assumes that there are right and just relationships among people, infringements of which will have disastrous consequences for the flourishing of the human community in general and persons in particular. Within the black church tradition, for instance, it would be difficult to overestimate the significance of "the Lord" as a divine title. It is "the Lord" who sustains and strengthens in time of need; it is "the Lord" who stands alongside those who suffer humiliation; it is "the Lord" who is the inveterate foe of oppression and the ultimate liberator from slavery.[19]

Within this constitutional heritage and with *Adonai* as author and guarantor, it is the specific and urgent message of the prophets constantly to recall the People of God not just to the living exercise of these values for themselves, but to the mission of God through them to the entire human community. As the title of *Adonai* is identified with the Messiah or Christ, the church is likewise called into this *missio Dei*. Audacious as is the Christian claim that Jesus Christ is to be addressed as *Adonai*, Lord, it is well for us to remember in the context of our Advent preparation the mission that Jesus claimed for himself: "Do not think that I have come to abolish the law and the prophets, I have come not to abolish but to fulfill."[20]

That these words occur within the context of the Sermon on the Mount following Jesus's articulation of the Beatitudes elucidating the conditions of life in God's reign is no accident. Such, then, is the character and pedigree of this focus on *Adonai* for the second Sunday of an expanded Advent season.

Advent 3: *Rex gentium* / *Christ the King Sunday* (November 20–26)

It is also no accident that the Great "O" Antiphon provides the focus for the third Sunday in an expanded Advent season. For this is the Sunday set since

---

19. This has been impressed upon me not simply through reading and media reporting, but by colleagues and students in the Colgate Rochester Crozer Divinity School's Black Church Studies program and, effectively, by direct experience through weekly worship in the black church tradition for over a decade and a half (1983–1999) while I was a dean and professor at that ecumenical seminary.

20. Matthew 5:17. It was important for Matthew's original Jewish audience to make the connection between Sinai and the Mount from which the body of chapter 5 was proclaimed. While this remains significant for contemporary Christians as well, it is also of note that the Matthean Gospel is the only one that explicitly mentions "church" (*ekklesia*).

1969 for the feast of Christ the King. Two items are immediately of note. The first is that the placing of *Rex gentium* (King of the nations) alters the original medieval order of the "O" Antiphons. The second is that this celebration was not from its 1925 inception observed on its present date in the liturgical year. Some significant matters about the character of the day can, nevertheless, be addressed through attention to the questions implicit in these two facts.

As we project the "O" Antiphons upon the larger canvas of an expanded Advent, it is well to reiterate that their original order was principally governed by a literary conceit: an acrostic arrangement of the initial from the name or title following the "O" so that it read *Ero cras* ("I shall be present tomorrow"). It was argued earlier in this chapter that while we may continue to appreciate the deeper point of Christ being all-in-all, it is not absolutely necessary to maintain the hidden medieval word play. In other words, what is lost by the rearrangement is only an arcane, and to modern sensibilities, obscure puzzle. More positively, it may be asserted that in this case the rearrangement serves in the present to give new life to what we have inherited from the long tradition.[21]

Here precisely, then, is the relevance of conjoining the "O" Antiphon designation of this Sunday with the Feast of Christ the King. As noted above, it is a solemnity of rather recent mint (1925) and even more recent alteration of date (1969). Originally, Pope Pius XI instituted the feast as a direct counter to the totalitarian claims of the modern state. The immediate threat in 1925 was, of course, communism on one hand, and the looming threat of fascism on the other. In more general terms, the annual celebration of this feast with its particular focus on the lordship as well as the universal and eternal scope of Christ's reign was promulgated to stand as a witness over against any and all secularizing tendencies of the contemporary world. Although there was an internal reason adduced for setting the feast on the last Sunday of October, there was a concomitant and perhaps unintended ecumenical offense in placing it on Reformation Sunday.

Given the occasions of its institution and in the face of the calamities of two world wars that reflected anything but the Kingdom of Christ, or

---

21. As previously noted, the *ero cras* acrostic arrangement of the "O" Antiphons was not universal. Recent research has shown, rather, a certain flexibility in their arrangement (and, as also noted, additions in some locales). Cf. especially Martin O'Connell, *Eternity Today: On the Liturgical Year*, vol. 1, *On God and Time: Advent, Christmas, Epiphany* (New York: Continuum, 2006), 73.

perhaps in spite of these cataclysms, the feast proved itself popular and last-ing. In the spirit of the ecumenical age ushered in by the establishment of the World Council of Churches in 1948 and the Second Vatican Council (1962–1964), Pope Paul VI not only reiterated the importance of the feast by raising it to the highest possible status—a solemnity—he also removed any taint of ecumenical offense by relocating its observance to its present date in November.[22] And, indeed, as previously noted, the celebration of this feast has become an ecumenical success story. In addition to the Roman Catholic Church, all traditions using the *Revised Common Lectionary* observe the day as the Reign of Christ / Christ the King.[23] Reordering the appearance of a particular Great "O" Antiphon is a heuristic move appropriate to the fact of this wide-spread observance: *Rex gentium* / King of Nations as the focus of the third Sunday of an expanded Advent season is totally congruent with the solemnity. Beyond that, the eschatological note prominent in either designa-tion is central: All worldly claims to ultimate loyalties are rendered relative. For Christians, reflecting on this is part and parcel of taking stock, both per-sonally and as a community, at the inception of a new year.

Advent 4: Radix Jesse / Root of Jesse Sunday (November 27–December 03)

With the fourth Sunday of Advent we literally get in touch with our Jewish roots. If, as was noted earlier, the People of God found their very constitu-tion as a community in a divine law directed toward justice and peace, then the purpose of the subsequent prophetic voices in their history was ever

---

22. There is an intriguing question about the original date set for this feast. In its establishing encyclical *Quas primas*, Pope Pius XI indicated the propriety of the date in this way: "The last Sun-day of October seemed the most convenient for this purpose, because it is at the end of the liturgical year, and thus the feast of the Kingship of Christ sets the crowning glory upon the mysteries of the life of Christ already commemorated during the year, and before celebrating the triumph of all the Saints [November 1], we proclaim and extol the glory of him who triumphs in all the Saints . . ." (13) The rationale adduced here seems to argue that the culmination or end of the liturgical year is the Feast of All Saints. Hence the last Sunday of the liturgical year would be the last Sunday of October. This may rest upon the fact that Pius XI came to the papal dignity from the archiepiscopal see of Milan, which always had observed (and still does) a longer Advent. But, then, perhaps not, since Paul VI came to the papacy by the same route and reconfigured the feast to the present date. In either case, however, the eschatological point of Christ the King is its central feature. (The English text of the cited encyclical can be found at http://w2.vatican.va/content/pius-xi-/en/encyclicals/documents/hf_p-xi_enc_11121925_quas_primas.html.)

23. This would include nearly all of the so-called mainline churches in the United States and Canada as well as a growing number of churches elsewhere in the world who have adopted the *RCL*.

and again to recall them *to* the Eternal One and *from* their many-faceted but always idolatrous sins. Reminding them that living not just in accordance with the letter of the law, but deeply into the spirit of their constitution as God's people, was the constant and urgent message of the prophets. The eschatological note of urgency attached to the prophetic proclamation is, in this regard, perhaps nowhere better set forth than in Isaiah. It is there also that the word of hope is anchored:

> A shoot shall come out from the stump of Jesse,
> and a branch shall grow out of his roots.
> The spirit of the LORD shall rest on him,
> the spirit of wisdom and understanding,
> the spirit of counsel and might,
> the spirit of knowledge and the fear of the LORD.
> His delight shall be in the fear of the LORD.[24]

The next verses set forth the character of the foreseen righteous scion of Jesse and then present the familiar vision of the peaceable Kingdom, looking toward its fulfillment: "they will not hurt or destroy on all my holy mountain; for the earth will be full of the knowledge of the Lord as the waters cover the sea." To that magnificent, not to say "down to earth," desideratum is added the verse that forms this particular "O" Antiphon as, for Christians, it refers to Jesus as the Christ:

> On that day the root of Jesse shall stand as a signal
> to the peoples; the nations shall inquire of him, and
> his dwelling shall be glorious.[25]

In evoking the long lineage of Jesus as coming through David from the "root of Jesse" there is both an appeal to the past as giving ancestral weight

---

24. Isaiah 11:1–3 (NRSV). As noted previously this passage is the source for enumerating the seven gifts of the Holy Spirit. In the original Hebrew text (MT) only six gifts were designated, but by a scribal doubling a seventh gift came into being in the Greek version (Septuagint, LXX) and that is the principal list used by Christians during the Church's first millennium and a half. These gifts are the ones given in baptism and evoked at other times of significance, for example, at ordinations with the singing of *Veni Creator Spiritus*.

25. Isaiah 11:10 (NRSV).

to the source and character of the Messiah, and an eschatological note that looks to a transformation of history and fulfillment of the promise embedded in the heritage. This, especially in regard to the passages cited, has been the subject of hymns and anthems that can further focus and enrich the celebration of the fourth Sunday of Advent. Some of this will, of course, be delineated in the subsequent chapter of resources for an expanded season, but here a foretaste might be mentioned.

This Sunday might be a perfect one for some presentation in the course of the liturgy from the children and youth of the church school. With the direction of teachers they may, for instance, during the first weeks of Advent have been engaged in constructing a version of the Jesse tree that details the ancestry of Jesus. Another possible venture would be the production of a pageant centered on the same theme—a kind of living Jesse tree. In any case, it would be an opportunity for a creative approach to theological literacy both for the church school and the adults of the congregation.[26]

Advent 5: Clavis David / Key of David Sunday (December 4–10)

In meditating on the character of these Advent Sundays as they are designated by the succession of Great "O" Antiphons, a certain two-fold pattern can be discerned. The first of these patterns is perhaps best described as a kind of alternating current between, on the one hand, the cosmic or universal and, on the other hand, the historical and particular. This alternation can occur between the Sundays themselves, for example, from the universal creating and sustaining *Sapientia* / Widsom to the historical *Adonai* / Lord who liberates a caste of slaves and constitutes them into a people. Or, again, a particular kingship stemming from the *Radix Jesse* / Root of Jesse to the unbounded rule of a *Rex gentium* / King of Nations. This first kind of alternating pattern can also occur within a single Sunday itself as we shall see in delving into the fifth Sunday of Advent as our present subject.

The second pattern that can be discerned in the succession of these Sundays is one internal to each. Its description, furthermore, will lead us directly

---

26. If the "Jesse pageant" option were exercised, this could replace the annual pressure for an ever-earlier Christmas pageant put on by Sunday school children. That pageant, in any case, is best left until around Epiphany so the pilgrimage of shepherds and magi appropriately cap the twelve days of the Christmas season and not infringe upon a proper observance of Advent.

into the character of Advent 5. This figure has to do with the energy released by the alternating current as time and eternity intersect.[27] Here as well as in the previous Christ-title *foci* there appear implications in the movement between the recalled past and the hoped-for future. Both of these time aspects exhibit salvific elements in themselves and, taken together, are both pertinent to the flourishing of the human community and human beings as intended by the Triune God with whom we are in communion through worship. When the alternating current operates along this past-future axis and is encountered in the present by the Eternal One, a cruciform pattern is revealed and crucial energies are released in the present. All of this is another way of calling attention to the principal eschatological focus of Advent.

The interplay of these two discernable patterns, mediated through the succession of Christ-title *foci* and the thematic three-year lectionary cycle for the liturgies of a seven-week season are capable of providing, like a splendid gem, endlessly fascinating facets for reflection of and illumination by the light. So, then, how are they at work on *Clavis David* / Key of David Sunday? In this case, the metaphor of "light" turns out to be directly pertinent.

Once again several prophetic texts undergird the "O" Antiphon. The principal ones are from a single source, Isaiah, but in several locations: chapters 22:22; 9:7; and 42:7.[28] These all refer to the Messianic heir to the Davidic kingship with an eschatological vision looking toward a fulfillment of well-being marked by justice and peace. This fulfillment will exhibit the power by which the "last enemy," death, is overcome (*cf.* 1 Cor.15:26). This collation of texts is directly echoed and given its christological point in the last book of the New Testament, also prophetic: "These are the words of the holy one, the true one, who has the key of David, who opens and no one will shut, who shuts and no one opens" (Rev. 3:7). Such considerations led to this "O" Antiphon's original composition as follows:

---

27. Here it is important to remember a distinction discussed in our first and second chapters, namely, that eternity is not to be conceived as time extended indefinitely, but, rather, as a quality appropriate to God that intersects with the temporal sequence, ever and at any point.

28. In order: "I will place on his shoulder the key of the house of David; he shall open, and no one shall shut; he shall shut, and no one shall open"; "His authority shall grow continually, and there shall be endless peace for the throne of David and his kingdom"; and "to open the eyes of the blind, to bring out the prisoners from the dungeon, from the prison those who sit in darkness" (all NRSV).

O Key of David and scepter of the House of Israel;
    you open and no one can shut; you shut and no one can open;
Come, and lead the prisoners from the prison house,
    those who dwell in darkness and the shadow of death.[29]

It can already be seen in the petition that follows the *Veni* of this antiphon that the prayer is more directed to Christ, who as righteous judge, will open rather than shut. Or, it may be that a bit more exegesis is appropriate. Such is the case with the translation based on the work of John Mason Neale in the nineteenth century and appearing in most contemporary hymnals. Here Christ appears as the one who opens heaven (the way of life) and shuts hell (the way of death). Thus we are enabled to come into the living light from the isolating dark of the grave:

O come, thou Key of David, come, and open wide our heavenly home;
make safe the way that leads on high, and close the path to misery.[30]

And it is precisely in that subtle turning from our human condition as ever under the "shadow of death" to the prospect of "eternal life" through the life and mission of Jesus Christ that the possibility is effectively brought to light. The presence of both the patterns articulated at the outset of this discussion are at play, then, on *Clavis David* / Key of David Sunday. The past prophetic hope is recalled and its future fulfillment are both made present. It is here also that the universal and particular meet. Liturgically this happens when our release from the "prison house" of sin and its wage, death, is proclaimed following prayers of confession:

Almighty God have mercy on you, forgive you all your sins through our Lord Jesus Christ, strengthen you in all goodness, and by the power of the Holy Spirit *keep you in eternal life*.[31]

---

29. *O clavis David, et sceptrum domus Israel; qui aperis, et nemo claudit; claudis, et nemo aperit: veni, et educ vinctum de domo carceris, sedentem in tenebris, et umbra mortis.* Cited in *The Hymnal 1982 Companion*, vol. 3 A, Raymond E. Glover, ed. (New York: Church Publishing, 1994), 103.

30. *The Hymnal 1982* (New York: Church Hymnal, 1982), hymn 56. It was always my early temptation as a cathedral choirboy (descant, in those halcyon days) to vocalize what must otherwise remain a sight rhyme and thus to sing "mih-zer-EYE" to correspond with the preceding "high" of the petition.

31. Book of Common Prayer (New York: Church Publishing, 1979), 360. Emphasis added to

Advent 6: Oriens / Morning Star Sunday (December 11–17)

As we near the end of the Advent season the theme of *light* in contrast to shadow begins to be prominently introduced. This was so in consideration of *Clavis David* Sunday and it is, by the very title of this *Oriens* Sunday, manifestly so. The increasing presence of this theme has effectively received silent confirmation in the liturgies of Advent by the growing light of candles lit on successive Sundays.[32] At least for those who live in our earth's northern hemisphere, we are in a season of decreasing daylight and long nights that will not even begin to invert that ratio until just a few days prior to Christmas.[33] But even where just the opposite case obtains, the growing external light of lengthening days in the southern half of our planet could be taken heuristically as a cosmic confirmation of the liturgical emphasis. Yet for those of us who await the winter solstice, the growing light in the Advent worship, thematic or tapered, shines out, serving as a counterpoint to the brevity of day.

As for the Christ-title linked to the sun, it is, once again, elucidated in the familiar words of the prophet: "the people who walked in darkness have seen a great light; those who lived in a land of deep darkness—on them light has shined" or, later, "Arise, shine, for your light has come and the glory of the Lord has dawned upon you . . . over you the Lord will rise and his glory will appear upon you."[34] This word receives further confirmation from the

---

underscore the point of being kept (now) in eternal life. This exemplifies the cruciform theology of the eternal as intersecting the temporal sequence ever and at any point. Although this may seem specific to the Episcopal Church, the formulation is typical of a general restatement in our age of early church theology in regard to time and eternity. To put a fine point on it, eschatology is rescued from a totally futuristic reference. For instance, the old BCP absolution ended, "strengthen you in all goodness, and *bring you to everlasting life* (that is, the prospect is future only and eternity is conceived as time extended; again, emphasis added).

32. Inevitably, when introducing the proposal of an expanded Advent to those responsible for planning, leadership, and evaluation of worship, the first question to arise normally comes from the head of the altar guild or flower committee, "But what about the Advent wreath?" This question is directly dealt with in Chapter 5 as it is focused on "Practical and Pastoral Concerns." Suffice it to say here that a seven-candle wreath is envisioned.

33. As one who has liturgical theologian friends in Australia, South Africa, Argentina, and Brazil, it has been impressed upon me in a vigorous way to remember that much if not most of Christian hymnography in conjunction with particular liturgical seasons assumes a northern clime. Thus singing in autumn about an Easter "spring of souls" becomes problematical. Likewise, in Advent, expanded or not, the "light/dark" theme must be handled with care.

34. Isaiah 9:2 and 60:1–3. The latter citation forms the beginning of the Morning Prayer canti-

last of the canonical prophets, Malachi: "But for you who revere my name the sun of righteousness shall rise, with healing in his wings."[35]

The original composers of the *Oriens* antiphon took up these themes, but also referenced their New Testament echoes and ratifications in Luke's Gospel and the Epistle to the Hebrews.[36] The divine eternal light (*splendor lucis aeternae*) was, of course, connected primordially with the theme of God's righteousness (*Sol justitiae*), but how does that come to be conjoined with the Messiah, the Christ as one who will "rise with healing in his wings," that is, ensure the blessing of peace as well?[37] That, of course, is the business of the New Testament writers and, specifically, the ones mentioned.

As the Christian tradition began its early development the mining of "the Scriptures" referred to in the Nicene Creed continued. A prominent example may be seen in regarding Psalm 80 as particularly appropriate to the Advent season, especially in the following refrain referencing salvific light, repeated three times in the course of its eighteen verses:

Restore us, O God of hosts; *
    show the light of your countenance and we shall be saved.[38]

Additionally, the venerable tradition of the church's hymnography has continued not only to make the connection but to enhance its meaning with ever-growing depth, breadth, and height of meaning. Thus, for instance, fast forwarding to a seventeenth-century hymn, "How Shall I Sing That Majesty Which Angels Do Admire?" we find not faint echoes but strong reverberations of these themes combined by the poet (and, indeed, all who sing it):

---

cle *Surge, illuminare* in the BCP 1979, 87–88. The canticle goes on to emphasize that in this divine light, peace and justice will be fulfilled and even the human need for the light of sun and moon will be surpassed: "The Lord will be your everlasting light, and your God will be your glory."

35. Malachi 4:2. In the Christian organization of the Bible, Malachi stands at the division point and thus, this announcement about the dawning of the "sun of righteousness," is at the very threshold of the New Testament. This placement was not, of course, accidental when early church leadership arranged the contents of Scripture.

36. Luke 1:79 (echoing Isaiah) and Hebrews 1:3 (establishing the Messiah's divinity at the outset).

37. The entire "O" Antiphon is: *O Oriens, splendor lucis aeternae, et sol justitiae: veni, et illumina sedentes in tenebris, et umbra mortis*: "O Daystar, splendor of eternal light and sun of righteousness: Come and illumine those who sit in darkness and the shadow of death." The "those who" is understood to be all of humanity.

38. BCP 1979, 702–703.

Enlighten with faith's light my heart, Inflame it with love's fire;
then shall I sing and bear a part with that celestial choir . . .
They sing because thou art their Sun; Lord send a beam on me;
For where heaven is but once begun, there alleluias be.[39]

Yet it is to the earliest of traditions that we may look for the definitive connection between *O Oriens* and the Christ-Messiah whose full manifestation we await in this season of expectation. For that we have direct reference to a singularly beautiful liturgical song traditionally sung by the deacon at the outset of the Great Vigil of Easter when the new light of the Paschal candle is processed in the darkness through the body of the congregation to its place of honor near the altar. This is, of course, the great hymn *Exsultet*, the call to "Rejoice!" in the victory of our God, the Christian Passover from death to life. That extended and ecstatic song concludes with the prayer:

Holy Father, accept our evening sacrifice, the offering of this candle in your honor. May it shine continually to drive away all darkness. May Christ, the Morning Star who knows no setting, find it ever burning—he who gives his light to all creation, and who lives and reigns for ever and ever. *Amen.*[40]

It is, in fact, the resurrection of Christ that sets the seal upon the thematic connections focused in the character of *Oriens* / Morning Star Sunday for Advent's penultimate week. The cosmic pattern is rendered concrete in the historical sequence and the eschatological pattern qualifies otherwise unredeemed history for all time to come.

---

39. The hymn is by John Mason (1646–97), a clergyman of the Church of England who came from a dissenting background and served most of his career as the parish priest of Water Stratford in northern Buckinghamshire. In this citation I have conflated the second half of the second verse with the first half of the first, not only to make the point but to save citation of the entire four verses. The last line cited hints at how liturgical praise opens the way to entering God's kingdom here and now. The final verse, quite remarkably for its age, makes the eschatological point that has been the burden of this entire chapter, namely, "Thou art a sea without a shore, a sun without a sphere; Thy time is now and evermore, Thy place is everywhere." This felicitous paean is a happy (in being less rigidly geometrical) paraphrase of the medieval scholastic definition of God as "a sphere whose center is everywhere and circumference nowhere" (that is, transcendent and unbounded). While Mason's hymn continues to be a feature of English hymnody, in North America it seems only to appear in the Anglican Church of Canada's *Common Praise* (1998).

40. Book of Common Prayer, 287.

Advent 7: Emmanuel / God with Us Sunday
(December 18–24)

As we saw in the first chapter, the lectionary which sets out the particular emphases of seasons and Sundays, now turns in this last Sunday of Advent from its long eschatological focus toward incarnation. It is only now that our Scripture readings prepare for our annual virtual pilgrimage to Bethlehem and the recounting of the events we celebrate from the coming of the shepherds in Luke on Christmas Eve to the arrival of the Gentile Magi twelve days later on the Epiphany. The actual time of this part of our pilgrimage varies each year during this last week and can be shorter or longer.[41]

In any case, though the lectionary now begins to point us toward Bethlehem, the last of the Great "O" Antiphons as a focus for *Emmanuel* Sunday keeps us decisively in the eschatological mode on that journey. In fact the whole skein of the antiphons is held together and aptly summarized at this critical turning point:

O Emmanuel, our king and our lawgiver, the hope of nations
and their savior: Come, and save us, Lord our God.[42]

The Christ-title, Emmanuel, is again rooted in the prophet Isaiah, but this time specifically applied by Matthew at the very beginning of the New Testament. Here, as that Gospel brings to conclusion the first chapter (the "begats," which hardly anyone now bothers to read), we enter into the dreamscape of Joseph when a divine messenger reveals to him that he should take Mary to wife, regardless of the situation, "for the child conceived within her is from the Holy Spirit." Then the dream is briefly interrupted as the narrator cites the relevant passage from the Isaiah:

All this took place to fulfill what had been spoken by the Lord through the prophet: "Look, the virgin shall conceive and bear a son, and they shall

---

41. This appears, for instance, in comparing the years 2016 and 2017. In 2016 an entire week separated the last Sunday of Advent from Christmas Day, which fell on Sunday. In 2017, by contrast, the last Sunday of Advent doubles as the day of Christmas Eve itself. Obviously, the actual distance from Nazareth to Bethlehem remains the same, but the virtual distance of the spiritual pilgrimage varies dramatically.

42. *O Emmanuel, Rex et legifer noster, exspectatio gentium, et salvator earum: Veni, et salvandum nos, Domine, Deus noster.*

name him Emmanuel," which means "God is with us." When Joseph awoke from sleep, he did as the angel of the Lord commanded him . . .[43]

The rest of the New Testament is, in an important sense, simply the unfolding or explication of that title Emmanuel, that is, God is with us in the person and work, the life and mission of Jesus Christ and the church as the Body of Christ under historical conditions. Here, too, the intertwined patterns that we have perceived throughout the season of an expanded Advent are once again exhibited. For while the historical development is set forth, the impenetrating, ever-present eschatological element is there as well. If we meet a nascent God-with-us at the outset of the first canonical book of the New Testament, we meet a fully matured God-with-us at its close. The cruciform conjunction reaches what we may justly call the omega-point in the final book of the Bible with this pertinent "last word" on the exegesis of *O, Emmanuel*:

> "See, the home of God is among mortals. He will dwell with them as their God; they will be his peoples, and God himself will be with them; he will wipe away every tear from their eyes. Death will be no more; mourning and crying and pain will be no more, for the first things have passed away." And the one who was seated on the throne said, "See, I am making all things new." Also he said, "Write this, for these words are trustworthy and true." Then he said to me, "It is done! I am the Alpha and the Omega, the beginning and the end."[44]

Conclusion

In this chapter we have been establishing and explicating the shape and feel, the structure and character of an expanded Advent. The focus has been on the application of the Messianic names or Christ-titles of the Great "O" Antiphons to the seven Sundays of the liturgical season. On the historical model of how those antiphons evolved from their monastic context to a wider usage through their hymn form, we are now suggesting their projection

---

43. Respectively, Isaiah 7:14 and Matthew 1:20–24 (both NRSV). Interestingly, the Isaiah passage is translated "young woman" while in Matthew the citation from the prophet is translated "virgin." The meeting of political correctness and piety may, perhaps, explain the difference.

44. Revelation 21:3b–6.

upon an even larger screen in service of re-imagining the season of Advent itself. In setting forth the character of these Sundays, and indeed the weeks following them, two patterns were discerned: one of alteration between the universal and the particular and the other revealing the present intersection of eternity with time along the sliding scale of past to future and vice versa. The aim has been to exhibit the richness of these focal themes, planting the suspicion that they may be inexhaustible.

We saw in the first chapter how the principal theme of such an Advent, taking its emphasis from the lectionary, is eschatological rather than incarnational. And, further, it was argued that eschatology itself in our age stands in need of restatement, liberating it from a confusion with apocalypticism as well as inadequate conceptions of time. This was particularly addressed as we attempted to explicate an eschatology related to worship and freed from the limitations of *eschata* (last things) in favor of the *eschaton* (full manifestation of the Reign of God / Kingdom of Christ). We observed also the implications for mission in these restatements and their liturgical connection:

> At the table we become one family. The future that God has in store for us is already breaking into the present. The risen Christ unites himself to us, gathering us in his name, incorporating us into his paschal mystery, filling us with his Spirit, and making us his body *for the world*.[45]

In the second chapter the discussion turned to an investigation of two major problems associated with an authentic observance of Advent. The first problem concerned the depredations perpetrated upon the Advent season by a global Christmas Culture. A corollary to this difficulty was found in the temptation for the church's complicity with that culture in observing Advent only as a preparation for Christmas holidays. An antidote not only to the culture, but especially for overcoming ecclesial complicity, was explored in the recovery of a lively sense of the possibilities of liturgical renewal and, more specifically, its challenge to the idols of culture.[46]

---

45. Thomas P. Rausch, S.J., *Eschatology, Liturgy, and Christology: Toward Recovering an Eschatological Imagination* (Collegeville, MN: Liturgical Press, 2012), 140. Emphasis added to underscore missional point.

46. Possibilities for the operation of a formation counter to that of the world and the power of liturgy over time to forward that end were particularly referenced from a voice in the Reformed

Now at the conclusion of this chapter concerned with the thematic emphasis of an expanded Advent as focused in its particular Sundays, we come to the point of asking, "What are the liturgical resources for sustaining and forwarding that emphasis and those *foci* over time for the worshiping assembly?" The pattern of the assembly's worship assumed in the next chapter presenting such resources is the classic four-fold eucharistic one of (1) Gather, (2) Word, (3) Table, and (4) Send. While many of the traditions observing the seasons of a liturgical year understand and practice a eucharistic celebration on the Lord's Day, it is recognized that some do not feature the element of Table or Holy Communion every Sunday. For these latter traditions not everything in the next chapter will be applicable weekly, but it is hoped that the way for adaptation or occasional use will be apparent. In any case, it is to setting forth those resources that we now turn.[47]

tradition by the work of James K. A. Smith, *Imagining the Kingdom: How Worship Works* (cf. Ch. 1, note 17) and his earlier volume *Desiring the Kingdom: Worship, Worldview, and Cultural Formation* (Cf. ch. 2, note 11). Both works are published by Baker Academic, Grand Rapids, MI, 2013 and 2009, respectively.

47. The Rev. Dr. Suzanne Duchesne, a Methodist member of the Advent Project Seminar, addresses some of the possiblities for traditions not featuring a celebration of Holy Communion every Sunday, following, rather, a common order of Protestant worship that virtually concludes with the sermon, offering, and a Sending Rite. A *précis* of her presentation can be found in *Proceedings* (Notre Dame, IN: NAAL, 2014), 32.

CHAPTER 4

Resources

How Can We Observe an Expanded Advent?

About Music

The resources presented in this chapter have been produced by individuals and working groups of the Advent Project Seminar in the North American Academy of Liturgy. With one exception they are set forth according to the four-fold design of the Sunday eucharistic assembly's worship: Gather, Word, Table, Send. The exception is the hymnody for the seven weeks of Advent. In order to present a comprehensive Index of Hymns across a wide variety of traditions, it was necessary to group these all together, rather than specified into the four movements of the worship pattern. The resultant work covering thirty-four hymnals from thirteen traditions proved too large for inclusion in this book. This index is, however, readily found as a downloadable resource reference online at www.churchpublishing.org/whatarewewaitingfor.[1]

It is important to stress at the outset of a chapter on resources the importance of music in worship. Music not only instrumentally frames but ecstatically infuses our worship. This is especially so as the individuals of a congre-

---

1. The seminar's Alphabetical Index of Hymns represents the work of a committee composed of the Rev. Dr. Elise A. Feyerherm (editor and final redactor), Dr. Carol A. Doran (music consultant to the Advent Project Seminar), and the author. One advantage of placing the index on our website, rather than in this chapter on resources, is that it can be more easily expanded and updated there.

gation are transformed into a chorus, one body or instrument, through the singing of the standard elements of the liturgy (*Kyrie, Gloria, Trisagion, Sursum corda, Sanctus,* and so on), and by joining together in voicing hymns that mark particular emphases of certain Sundays and seasons. What is revealed through such reflections is that music is essential to worship, that is, sung liturgy is the norm, said liturgy a diminution. It has been well-said that Christians believe what they sing, or, more classically, to sing is to pray twice. Those responsible for worship planning, conduct, and evaluation will find a vital resource in the "Alphabetical Index of Hymns" for the Advent season.

For those in parishes or congregations charged with planning for worship, the index of hymns will provide resources both within and across various traditions. Most helpfully, the index adds a feature that marks certain hymns as appropriate to one or another specific week of the seven week season according to the Sunday "O" antiphon designations set forth in Chapter 3. Selections will, however, have to be made for the various movements of the liturgy. In using the index, worship planners will find it necessary to make choices about which specific texts and tunes will serve, for instance, as processional, gradual, offertory, communion, or sending hymns.

Gathering

Perhaps the most important consideration of the Gathering Rite at the inception of Advent and the new liturgical year is avoidance of what in effect is often two or three "gatherings" instead of an integrated one. The principal challenge, as given pointed illustration in Chapter 2, is how to integrate the blessing of the Advent wreath and the lighting of its first candle into this part of the rite without duplication or confusion of purpose or theme. Normally, of course, the worshiping assembly congregates some minutes before the start of service. This time is usually accompanied by an organ or instrumental prelude.[2] Most often the commencement of the liturgy is marked by a musical pause, followed by a lively entrance or processional hymn.[3]

---

2. In some traditions this congregating time provides occasion for greetings of pew or seat mates, while in others it is marked by a preparatory period of meditative silence or personal prayer. Either mode can serve a gathering purpose, especially if the former is not too distracting, nor the latter custom perceived as indifference.

3. The order and amplitude of Gathering Rites varies across traditions, for example the Roman rite after the greeting ("The grace of our Lord Jesus Christ . . ."), followed by necessry liturgial

At this point, however, it might be well to introduce something that will mark the season and the start of the year as different from the usual. The entering ministers (sanctuary party) could be gathered prior to the processional (along with the choir) at the rear of the nave. The service bulletin could indicate in print that those who are able should stand when the sound of a chime is heard and the Presider could initiate the opening doxological greeting (call to worship) from that location. In the Episcopal Church, as has been previously noted, this greeting is apt for the central theme of Advent, namely,

Presider	Blessed be God, Father, Son, and Holy Spirit.
People	**And blessed be God's kingdom, now and forever. Amen.**

In any case, such beginnings would be followed by any supplemental prayer and an Advent hymn of praise during the procession.[4] This pattern could be maintained throughout the season. On the first Sunday, however, the sanctuary party would make what is called "a station" at the place where the Advent wreath is located.[5]

Here, then, is a suggested rite of blessing for the wreath that includes the lighting of its first candle:

---

announcements, features options among Trinitarian doxologies, the possibility of a penitential rite, then on to *Kyrie, Gloria,* and Opening Prayer (Collect of the Day); while the ten eucharistic settings for Lutherans in the *ELW* feature two options for a penitential/thanksgiving for baptism rite, while in others offering much the same pattern beginning with the Grace and different musical settings (with one in Spanish) for an opening dialogical intercession and the *Gloria* or hymn of praise, ending with the Prayer of the Day (Collect); the Methodist *Book of Worship* (while following this general pattern, *cf.* 33), puts the traditional Collect for the day as the first item in the Liturgy of the Word; and finally the Presbyterian *Common Worship* puts a "Call to Worship" first, followed by the Prayer of the Day (Collect) and concluding with a Hymn of Praise and the option of a Confession, Pardon and Peace with a canticle/psalm/spiritual transition to the Liturgy of the Word. With such variations, the general pattern of Gathering Rites is similar for all.

4. In the Episcopal Church this arrangement would serve to avoid what in effect is a duplication in the Gathering Rite with a processional hymn followed almost immediately by the *Gloria in excelsis,* thus providing two hymns of praise. Though with Advent no longer regarded as a penitential season in the same way as Lent, singing the *Gloria* is permissible, it would be best to refrain from it for a while so that its reappearance at Christmas is enhanced.

5. This is analogous, for instance, to the stop customarily made after the processional hymn (usually *Adeste fideles*) by the sanctuary party at the *crèche* during the Christmas Eve liturgy to bless it and, in some cases, to place a representation of the Christ child in the manger crib. Incidentally, the *crèche* should not appear until Christmas Eve.

Blessing of the Advent Wreath and Lighting of the First Candle
First Sunday of Advent (*Sapientia* / Wisdom Sunday)

At their entry into the chancel for the celebration of the Holy Eucharist, the Presider (and other ministers) may make a station where the Advent wreath is located. The following versicles and responses are said before the blessing of the wreath.

Presider   The Lord has made known his victory,
People   *God's righteousness is shown to the nations.*
Presider   In righteousness shall God judge the world.
People   *And all the peoples in peace and equity.*

If holy water has been used during the procession to bless the people, some of that water is also sprinkled upon the wreath as the Presider says the following prayer.

Holy and Eternal One, giver of life and light, bless we pray you this ring of evergreen and circle of candles, that as our way is illumined in this season by the growing radiance of Christ, so also we may be firmly grounded in your constant love; through Jesus Christ our Lord, who lives and reigns with you and the Holy Spirit, one God, now and for ever. *Amen.*

The blessing concludes with the lighting of the first candle on the wreath during which the following is sung or said.

Presider   O Lord, how manifold are your works!
People   *In wisdom you have made them all.*

The following canticle is then sung or said three times as the Presider and other ministers proceed to their accustomed positions.
    Holy God,
    Holy and Mighty,
    Holy Immortal One,
    Have mercy upon us.

The Gathering Rite concludes with the Collect for the First Sunday of Advent and the service continues with the Liturgy of the Word.[6]

Collects (Prayer of the Day/Themes) for an Expanded Advent

The following seven collects were composed by the author. They can also be found on the Advent Project website under "Resources" and may be freely used with attribution. If congregations wish to use the standard collects of their respective traditions at the transition from the Gathering Rite, these collects can alternatively serve elsewhere in the liturgy, for instance, at the conclusion of the Prayers of the People according to the particular Sunday of the season.

Advent 1: Sapientia (Wisdom) Sunday

Eternal God, your Word of wisdom goes forth and does not return empty: Grant us such knowledge and love of you that we may perceive your presence in all creation and every creature; through Jesus Christ our Lord, who with you and the Holy Spirit lives and reigns, now and for ever. *Amen.*

---

6. Here is a brief commentary on the blessing. The opening versicles and responses are paraphrases of verses 3 and 10 of Ps. 98 *Cantate Domino*, "Sing to the Lord a new song"—appropriate to the beginning of a new year and the Advent themes relating to God's righteous judgment of the world. This Psalm, by the way, is the one which Isaac Watts paraphrased into the hymn "Joy to the World" (cf. Chapter 2).

The use of baptismal water at the beginning of the season to link the congregation with the blessing of the Advent wreath seems appropriate, but can be reduced to using water from the font to bless the wreath alone, or not using water at all, letting the words of prayer suffice without any sign of blessing.

The prayer itself twice expands God's gift of 'life and light', first to link 'evergreen' to life and light to the seven candles, and then theologically to link what will be the growing light of the candles during the successive Sundays to the radiance of the risen and glorified Christ as the full manifestation of God's eternal and life-giving love.

The versicle and response during the lighting of the first candle is a direct citation of verse 25 from Ps. 104 *Benedic, anima mea*, "Bless the Lord, O my soul."

Most traditions supply musical versions of the great Orthodox hymn *Trisagion*. This canticle as part of the gathering rite during Advent not only appropriately reserves the *Gloria in excelsis* to the Christmas-Epiphany season, but serves also to reserve the *Kyrie, eleison* (customarily interpreted as penitential) to the season of Lent.

Advent 2: Adonai (Lord of Might) Sunday

O Lord our God, you gave your law that righteousness might abound: Put it into our hearts to love justice for others as much as we desire it for ourselves, that, as we know you to be our judge, so we may welcome your reign as it is manifested through Jesus Christ our savior; to whom, with you and the Holy Spirit, be dominion and praise for ever and ever. *Amen*.

Advent 3: Rex Gentium (Christ the King) Sunday

Lord Jesus Christ, in wisdom you order all things peaceably, and where you are sovereign justice prevails; so form our minds and rule our hearts that we may freely show your care in perfect service toward the common good; for with the Father and the Holy Spirit you live and reign, one God, now and for ever. *Amen*.

Advent 4: Radix Jesse (Root of Jesse) Sunday

Almighty God, you brought forth a royal branch from the ancient stock of Jesse's line: Grant that we who have been grafted into this heritage may bear fruit worthy of Jesus Christ; who with you and the Holy Spirit lives and reigns, one God, now and forever. *Amen*.

Advent 5: Clavis (Key of) David Sunday

Gracious God, your Son Jesus Christ opened wide the gate of heaven, making plain the way that leads to eternal joy: Grant that we who have been buried with Christ in baptism and raised to new life may strive courageously for the freedom and peace of the world; through the same your Son, Jesus Christ, to whom with you and the Holy Spirit be praise and dominion for ever and ever. *Amen*.

Advent 6: Oriens (Morning Star) Sunday

Lord Jesus Christ, in your resurrection you appeared as the Morning Star that knows no setting: Dawn upon the darkness of the human heart so that the deathly orders of this world may be overcome and your whole creation renewed; for with the Father and the Holy Spirit, you live and reign, one God, for ever and ever. *Amen*.

Advent 7: Emmanuel Sunday

Eternal God, you do not abandon us in exile but hear our plea for returning and rest: Visit us we pray with your presence and raise us to greet with hope and joy the promised day of salvation; through Jesus Christ, who with you and the Holy Spirit, lives and reigns now and for ever. *Amen.*[7]

Liturgy of the Word

The central resource for this part of the liturgy is, of course, the lectionary that has already received extensive presentation both in Chapter 1 and the online Appendices 1–3 with their thematic *préces* or summaries of particular readings and psalms.[8] Also, the online "Index of Hymns" will provide resources for music to be sung either in response to those lections or as the Gospel book is processed into the midst of the congregation for its proclamation.

A rich trove of resources for the sermons or homilies of an expanded Advent is, then, provided by the lectionary. Additionally, the thematic emphases of the particular Sundays focused on the Messianic names of Christ provide yet another resource that can aid the preacher in forwarding the continuing formation of that eschatological imagination so vitally important, not only for the Advent season itself, but also throughout the liturgical year. Finally, preachers of all ages and traditions will be able to bring to their homilies or sermons pertinent illustrative examples from both life experience and art—including literature, visual or aural media, and cinema.

The final portion of the Liturgy of the Word, of course, appears as the worshiping community's response to the proclamation of God's word

---

7. Though the above prayers are offered here without commentary, their congruence with the traditional form of such collects should be evident as well as their constant allusion to Scripture and the themes of the Advent season as set forth in previous chapters.

8. Inevitably, the question will arise about whether it would not be better to begin an expanded Advent with the readings for that whole year of the lectionary cycle rather than using the readings appointed for the last three weeks of the previous year for the first three Sundays of an expanded Advent. The advantages (many) of this have been addressed by an AP Seminar member. The Rev. Dr. W. Richard Hamlin in "Adjusting the Lectionaries for Continuity and Coherence during an Expanded Advent: A Feasibility Study," a *précis* of which appears in *Proceedings* (Notre Dame, IN: North American Academy of Liturgy, 2016), 31.

through Scripture, song, and sermon. This response is most appropriately referenced as the Prayers of the People. In most traditions, moreover, these intercessory/pastoral prayers follow a similar outline or pattern while the forms vary widely:

> *Prayer is offered with intercession for:*
> *The Universal Church, its members and mission*
> *The Nation and all in authority*
> *The welfare of the world*
> *The concerns of the local community*
> *Those who suffer and those in any trouble*
> *The departed (with commemoration of a saint when appropriate)*[9]

Ordinarily the Prayers of the People are led by a lay minister who serves in this capacity. Often these persons have received special training for the task or are drawn from a group within the congregation who have been charged with the weekly ministry of choosing, compiling, or even composing the intercessory prayer as well as leading it. Whatever the case may be in this regard, the placement of that person for this ministry during the liturgy is an important consideration. All-too-frequently the prayers are led facing the people from a lectern or ambo. This has the unfortunate effect of conveying the feeling that the prayers are being addressed to the people or that, regardless of their response, announcements are being made to them when it comes to specific occasions or persons included in the intercessions. A better practice would be to place the leader of the Prayers of the People in the midst of the assembly, preferably at the very spot from which the Gospel was proclaimed, but with the leader now facing the altar/table as representing the people. Such a choreography would not only underscore that the intercessions are coming from the midst of the assembly, but also that they are, in fact, a response by the congregation's having been formed in the Word that has been previously proclaimed.[10]

---

9. BCP 1979, 359.

10. Practically speaking, it should represent no great logistical hurdle to provide these lay ministers with a clip-on hearing loop microphone, since most congregations of any size are equipped for such hearing amplification. It has already been noted that the Presider concludes these prayers with an appropriate collect. If the seven particular Advent collects for Sundays have not been already used, they may fittingly be used as the concluding collect here.

In regard to the form of the Prayers of the People, there are many possibilities available through specific options authorized in the liturgical books of various tradition. Alternatively, others may be readily found on the internet. Here, as specific resources for an expanded Advent, two possibilities are offered. The first is to employ throughout the season a specific form of the Prayers of the People with the assembly's responses pertinently drawn from the Great "O" antiphons that designate particular Advent Sundays. Thus:

[The Deacon or other person appointed as Intercessor leads the prayers; the people respond as indicated.]
Brothers and sisters, as we joyfully await the full manifestation of God's reign in Christ, let us pray for the needs of the church and the world.

O Wisdom, you come forth from the mouth of the Most High and reach from beginning to end, mightily and sweetly ordering all things. Behold and bless your church, remembering especially [*Name*] our presiding bishop/primate, [*Name(s)*] our priest(s), [*Names*] our wardens, our vestry and delegates, and the people and clergy of the Church in [Anglican Cycle of Prayer for the day] and [Diocesan Cycle of Prayer and/ or partner churches]. Be present in ordering the life of this and every congregation.

Come and teach us the way of prudence.

O Adonai, God of the Covenant, ruler of the house of Israel, you appeared to Moses in the fire of the burning bush and on Mount Sinai gave your law. Forgive us when we stray from your guidance and will.

Come and redeem us for our life together.

O Root of Jesse, you stand as an ensign to humankind; before you rulers will shut their mouths, and nations bow in worship: We pray for your peace and justice in every nation and throughout the world; be present to all whose lives are ravaged by war and strife; especially we hold before you those from among us who serve our country abroad:

[*Name(s)*]. Guide the leaders of this and every land into the paths of peace and goodwill.

Come save us and do not delay.

O Key of David, and scepter of the house of Israel, you open and no one can shut, you shut and no one can open: Guide us in opening the doors of opportunity for the unemployed, for the homeless, for prisoners, and for all who are oppressed; and lead us in closing the doors that lead to poverty, bigotry, and injustice.

Come and bring the captives out of the prison house.

O King of the Nations and their Desire, you are the cornerstone that makes us one: We lift up all who are suffering and in need, especially. . . . Tend the sick, give rest to the weary, bless the dying, soothe the suffering, pity the afflicted, shield the joyous and help us minister to them in your love.

Come and save us whom you have fashioned out of clay.

O Dayspring, radiance of the Light Eternal and Sun of Righteousness: Shine your light on those who have died; remember especially those we now name. . ., and bring comfort to all those who mourn.

Come and enlighten all who sit in darkness and the shadow of death.

O Emmanuel, God with us, Expected One and Saviour, we give thanks for all the blessings of this life; for all those who today celebrate birthdays [*Name(s)*] and anniversaries [*Name(s)*]; and for the other blessings we now name silently or aloud [*pause*]. We thank you for the witness of all your holy ones (and especially Saint...whom we commemorate today). Make us all and everyone ready to receive you into our hearts, to serve you in all whom we meet, and to greet you in the fullness of your glory in the day of your appearing.

Come and save us, O Lord our God.

[The Presider concludes with an appropriate collect. If the BCP collects have been used as the collect for the day, then the one for a particular Sunday from among the seven week Advent prayers may be used here.][11]

If it appears desirable to use a variety of Prayers of the People during an expanded Advent by employing set forms found in the liturgical books of various traditions, then the following responses may be employed instead of those published. These would come on particular Sundays and replace the responses after each set of petitions.

Advent 1

Intercessor God of Wisdom, Lord Christ.
People *Hear us, we pray.*

Advent 2

Intercessor Mighty and merciful One, Lord Christ.
People *Hear us, we pray.*

Advent 3

Intercessor Sovereign God, Lord Christ.
People *Hear us, we pray.*

Advent 4

Intercessor Root of Jesse, Lord Christ.
People *Hear us, we pray.*

Advent 5

Intercessor Key of David, Lord Christ.
People *Hear us, we pray.*

---

11. These Prayers of the People were originally adapted from a United Church of Christ source by the Rev. David Smith for use specifically at St Luke's Episcopal Church, Fairport, NY. After further editing by the author they are offered for general use throughout the Episcopal Church and the Anglican Church of Canada. It should be clear how they may be adapted with further editing for even wider use in other traditions.

Advent 6

Intercessor Morning Star, Lord Christ.
People   *Hear us, we pray.*

Advent 7

Intercessor Emmanuel, Lord Christ.
People   *Hear us, we pray.*

As indicated, these responses could also be replaced by responses found in Prayers of the People downloaded from internet resources.

Liturgy of the Table

Following the reforms of Vatican II and specific elements of liturgical renewal it became possible for traditions using a single Great Thanksgiving to employ a variety of these eucharistic prayers, or conversely for traditions that had used nothing in this regard beyond translations of Jesus's words of institution at the Last Supper to enrich the Liturgy of the Table with more substantial prayers. In either case, these Great Thanksgivings clearly set forth elements recounting salvation history, calling to mind Jesus's identification of himself with the bread and wine (*anamnesis*), invocation of the Holy Spirit over the gifts (*epiclesis*), and supplication. Though this is the principal portion of the liturgy assigned to the presider, the assembly is called upon for participation at the beginning (*Sursum corda*, "Lift up you hearts" through *Sanctus & Benedictus*, "Holy, holy, holy"); again at midpoint, voicing those acclamations that conclude the *anamnesis*; and at the end by singing or saying the Great Amen.

In all of this there is one variable part according to the liturgical season or specific observance. This is the Proper Preface that is inserted by the presider just following the *Sursum corda* that gives further notice and application of the themes for the season or observance that are more fulsomely articulated by the Collect in the Gathering Rite and throughout the Liturgy of the Word. As resources specific to an expanded Advent, two such prefaces are offered here along with traditional chant settings. Thus:

A Proper Preface for Advent 1–4

It is right, and a good and joyful thing, always and everywhere to give thanks to you, Father Almighty, Creator of heaven and earth.

Because in Jesus Christ you established your reign of righteousness and peace, giving us partnership in its manifestation and hope for its fulfillment. Therefore, (and so on to the Sanctus) . . .

A Proper Preface for Advent 1 - 4

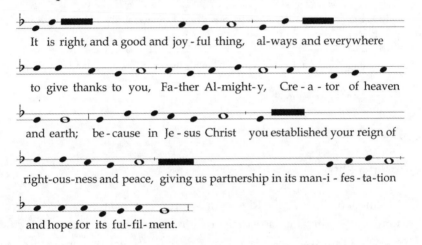

It is right, and a good and joy-ful thing, al-ways and everywhere to give thanks to you, Fa-ther Al-might-y, Cre-a-tor of heaven and earth; be-cause in Je-sus Christ you established your reign of right-ous-ness and peace, giving us partnership in its man-i-fes-ta-tion and hope for its ful-fil-ment.

A Proper Preface for Advent 5–7

It is right, and a good and joyful thing, always and everywhere to give thanks to you, Father Almighty, Creator of heaven and earth.

Because in your Son, Jesus Christ, you came among us in great humility that the whole human family created in your image might be redeemed from all ills and live in peace by the power of your love. Therefore, (and so on to the *Sanctus*) . . .[12]

---

12. There is ample precedent in the provision of more than one Proper Preface in a single season. During the forty days of Lent, for instance, there is a penitential one appropriate for the early weeks, another for weeks nearing the Paschal feast, and a third for Holy Week itself. These two Advent prefaces provide both for focus on the Reign of God / Kingdom of Christ and the later beginnings of a transition to the Christmas-to-Epiphany season.

A Proper Preface for Advent 5 - 7

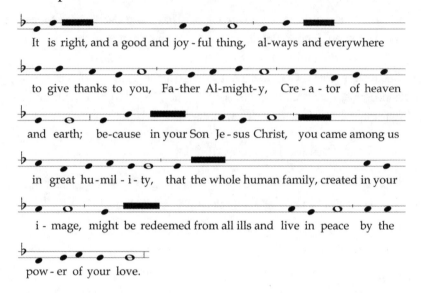

It is right, and a good and joy - ful thing, al-ways and everywhere
to give thanks to you, Fa-ther Al-might-y, Cre - a - tor of heaven
and earth; be-cause in your Son Je - sus Christ, you came among us
in great hu - mil - i - ty, that the whole human family, created in your
i - mage, might be redeemed from all ills and live in peace by the
pow - er of your love.

Sending Rite

One element of the Sending Rite seems appropriate for an expanded Advent season beyond the standard items of Post-Communion Prayer, Sending Hymn, and Dismissal. And that is a specific but optional Trinitarian blessing of the eucharistic assembly. Here is an example:

The Blessing

May Christ, the Wisdom of God, keep you steadfast in faith;

May Christ, most merciful Sovereign, sustain you in hope;

May Christ, Sun of Righteousness, perfect you in love;

And the blessing of the Eternal One, Father, Son, and Holy Spirit,

be upon you and remain with you always.

(or this)

And the blessing of the Holy Trinity, One God, be upon you
this day and for ever. *Amen*.

The three initial parts of this blessing reference several of the Messianic titles of Christ that are thematic for an expanded Advent (Wisdom, Sovereign, Morning Star) and the blessing's application of the effects of those titles in that order exemplify the three-fold office of Christ as prophet, king, and priest (the traditional *triplex munus Christi*). Perhaps the most familiar reference to the doctrine is found in the common hymn "Songs of thankfulness and praise" in the second verse where the *triplex* is specifically declared: "Manifest at Jordan's stream, Prophet, Priest, and King supreme."[13]

And with that musical reference final attention in this chapter is now called once again to the Alphabetical Index of Hymns for the season to be found online. This wide selection of hymns is listed alphabetically by first lines. As an aid to worship planners, and especially church musicians, they are also classified in two further ways: first by location(s) in the thirty-four hymnals presently referenced, and second, by weeks (again sometimes multiple) in an expanded Advent to which any particular hymn is especially pertinent by congruity with lectionary themes. Though most traditions will naturally employ only their own hymnals or supplementary musical resources, it may be helpful for church musicians to expand a particular congregation's awareness, and the choir's repertoire, by using hymns from other traditions or communities as anthems.

---

13. The text is cited here from the Episcopal Church's *Hymnal 1982*, (NY: Church Publishing, 1985), #135.

CHAPTER 5

Concerns

How Can Practical and Pastoral Questions Be Met?

This concluding chapter will respond to several practical questions and/or pastoral concerns in regard to the implementation of an expanded Advent. They range over such items as the Advent wreath; an expanded Advent and annual stewardship campaigns; the season and Sunday church school; how to handle years in which All Saints' Sunday coincides with Advent 1; and, finally, matters of congregational participation in trial usage. While a few of these questions (for example, the coincidence of Advent 1 and All Saints' Sunday) are denomination-specific, most of the concerns cross traditions.

The Advent Wreath

Given its ubiquity, it is perhaps inevitable that the first question to arise about a seven-week Advent is voiced by sometimes anguished altar guild leaders, *"But what about the Advent wreath?"* At least this has been the experience of members of the Advent Project Seminar in making presentations about trial use of an expanded season to clergy, church musicians, and worship committees. The question is rendered even more complex by the plethora of para-liturgical ceremonies that have inserted themselves into the Gathering Rite of the Sunday worshiping assembly.[1]

---

1. Some of these rites are officially authorized, but for the most part they are not. Most of them are not grounded in the integrity of the season but as previewing Christmas. The Advent Project's

Maintaining the integrity of the Gathering Rite has already been discussed in Chapter 4, but the insertion of the para-liturgies that have grown up around the Advent wreath are rooted, unfortunately, in a view of the season as a late-coming count-down to Christmas. The rubrics of the Roman rite, recognizing the home-devotional origins of the wreath prior to its appearance in ecclesial settings, restrict the use of such rites.[2] Similar instructions, though briefer, are echoed in the Episcopal Church's *Book of Occasional Services*.[3]

To all this is added another source of confusion around the color of the candles on the wreath. Some congregations surround a central white candle with three purple candles and a rose candle. The rose candle recognizes *Gaudete* Sunday at the beginning of the third week in the presently truncated Advent. Other traditions symbolize a post-penitential reading of Advent with four more joyously blue candles surrounding the central white candle.[4]

Beyond these considerations is the fact that in certain traditions, particularly Protestant ones, abstract names—Hope, Peace, Joy, Love—have attached themselves to the candles. All of these, it must be said, are reflective of aspirations appropriate for Christians at the start of a new liturgical year

---

director of resources, Dr. Laura E. Moore, addressed these para-liturgies in a seminar paper, "What to do about the Advent wreath? Or, not letting the tail wag the dog," *Proceedings* (Notre Dame, IN: NAAL, 2012), 36.

2. "Rubrics Concerning the Advent Wreath," *Book of Blessings* (Collegeville: Order of St. Benedict, Inc., 1989), chapter 47, "Order for blessing of an Advent Wreath (First Sunday in Advent)," ¶¶ 1509–1516. The book was prepared by the International Commission on English in the Liturgy, confirmed by the Apostolic See and authorized by various national Conferences of Catholic bishops. The operative rubric is: "When the Advent Wreath is used in church, on the Second and succeeding Sundays of Advent the candles are lighted either before Mass begins or immediately before the opening prayer; *no additional rites or prayers are used*. Emphasis added.

3. "Concerning the Advent Wreath," *Book of Occasional Services 2003* (New York: Church Publishing, 2004), 30, *viz.* "When it is used in the church, no special prayers or ceremonial elaboration . . . is desirable. At morning services the appropriate number of candles is lighted *before the service begins*" (emphasis added). Sad to say, this rubric is more honored in the breach than in the observance.

4. While long tradition is not to be lightly or unadvisedly dismissed, it does seem strange to maintain purple candles for the wreath since Advent is no longer a penitential season on the model of a mini-Lent. Also, the season does not, therefore, require a "refreshment" Sunday symbolized by a third-week rose candle. Relaxation from the rigors of a penitentially constructed season is no longer necessary. There is, however, every reason on the basis of the lectionary to keep the Sunday name drawn from the medieval introit *Gaudete* ("Rejoice!" or "Be joyful!").

as well as thematically pertinent to Advent. One further advantage to the attachment of such names to the candles of the wreath is that the practice has served to affirm the integrity of the season itself by stepping away from a culturally-induced "count-down to Christmas" mentality. The limitation to four such candles, however, disappears with a seven-week season. It may not, in fact, be necessary to designate the candles at all with such abstractions, but simply to let the lights for particular Sundays ordered according to the Great "O" antiphons symbolize the growing radiance of Christ as they are progressively lit to mark the weeks of the season.

By now it will be clear the following arrangement is envisioned for the Advent wreath: six blue candles grouped on the wreath around a white one in the center. Placement of the wreath can vary. In a cruciform church, it is possible, for instance, to suspend a ring from the central arch over the steps transitioning from the nave to the choir/pavement area. This would, of course, preclude a central candle so that a white candle, prominently placed, would have to join the six blue ones on the circle of the wreath. More usually, however, the wreath will be placed on a stand in the sanctuary somewhat to the left of the altar as the congregation views it. In either case, proportionality of the wreath itself to the architecture of the worship space is an important consideration.

Among visuals from congregations already participating in the observance of an expanded Advent, another possibility for placement of the wreath can be illustrated. In the following photograph, it will be noticed that the Advent wreath meets the test of proportionality for a large building. Placement of the wreath is on the congregation's right, but not in the altar area (which is at least visually distant). Here the seven-candle wreath has been placed in plain sight on the nave floor just at the steps leading up to the choir and sanctuary. The picture on the left gives a sense of size. The picture on the right shows the wreath's placement at the said location and just below the impressive lectern.

*Steps from cathedral nave to choir and sanctuary,
flanked by pulpit and lectern.*

Placement of Advent wreath near steps at foot of lectern.[5]

---

5. The author's photos were taken on Advent 3 (Christ the King Sunday) 2013 at Christ's Church Cathedral (Diocese of Niagara, Anglican Church of Canada), Hamilton, ON.

For those with crafting abilities, here are some specifications: the candles of this wreath are made of 4 x 4-inch wood stock with the edges of each candle beveled at a 45-degree angle. Six of the upright blocks have been painted blue and one white. The tops of the uprights have a circle routed out of them to the depth and diameter of a tea-light candle. The white candle for *Emmanuel Sunday* has been made three inches taller than the blue ones. The tea-light candles can be replaced as necessary by the altar guild prior to services during the season.[6]

Since the Advent wreath essentially made its way into the church, as indicated, from a home-based devotional practice for families, households, or communities, it seems fitting to conclude this section with an example shown above of a home wreath for the expanded season.

Six blue and one white ceramic tea-light candle holders are featured. Candles are lighted sequentially (and are replaced as necessary). A brief home liturgy can be found online at www.theadventproject.org. The service

---

6. The altar guild should also be responsible for the removal of the Advent wreath prior to the first services of Christmas Eve day. The last candle will have been lit on Advent 7. As liturgical theologian J. Neil Alexander remarks, "Its presence as a ritual fixture during Christmas is confusing at best." *Celebrating Liturgical Time: Days, Weeks, and Seasons* (New York: Church Publishing International, 2014), 45.

can be used any time, but is especially appropriate just prior to the Sunday evening meal when the family, household, or community is gathered and a new week's candle is lighted.

Advent and Stewardship Campaigns

In preparation for a new year, many congregations will have completed their annual fund or stewardship campaigns by the end of October. Perhaps just as many, however, will carry those efforts into the first weeks of November. The question addressed here is thus a practical one that arose from an Advent Project Workshop sponsored by the liturgical commission in the Episcopal Church's Diocese of Southern Ohio. The general question has to do with the relationship between the Reign of God / Kingdom of Christ and steward-ship. While the question was raised at the workshop specifically with regard to the Episcopal Church, this response can be more widely applied across traditions.[7]

1. Centrality of the Reign of God

In setting before us Jesus as the Christ or incarnate Word of God, the Gospel in general discloses him as proclaiming the Reign of God (sometimes referred to as the Kingdom of Christ, cf. Nicene Creed: Christ "seated at the right hand of the Father, and his kingdom will have no end"). Each of the four Gospels, in particular, is divided into two major parts: (1) Jesus's public ministry and (2) his passion. Mark begins directly with the public ministry; Matthew and Luke, of course, add their very different preliminary nativity stories; and John has a rather cosmic prologue about Jesus, compacting the nativity into a single phrase: "and the Word was made flesh and dwelt among us" (John 1:14 RSV).

During Jesus's public ministry, three main themes stand out. First, in Jesus's teaching, the values of God's Reign in contrast to those of "this world" are set forth in the parables. Second, Jesus's acts of healing exhibit signs of the Kingdom's character as promoting the flourishing of human community

---

7. To general interest among the attending forty or so clergy and lay leaders, the question was raised by the chair of the annual stewardship campaign for Christ Church Cathedral, Cincinnati. She indicated that there was some interest in observing an expanded Advent, but was soliciting theological grounding for the two foci of stewardship and the expanded season.

and well-being. And third, the accessibility of the Kingdom here and now is constantly reiterated by Jesus's reference to it as *near, at hand,* or *among you.* In sum, the public ministry persistently puts before Jesus's hearers (then, in the meanwhile, now, and for those yet to come) the challenge of choice regarding these values (for example, "you cannot serve God and money"), signs (for example, "do you wish to be healed?"), and accessibility (for example, "you are not far from the Kingdom of God").[8]

If the public ministry expresses, exhibits, and expects the Reign of God, it is Jesus's passion—from arrest and trial to execution and resurrection— that *enacts* the Kingdom and, by so doing, establishes it *in and for* the human community. Another way of saying this is that Jesus's passion shows the lengths to which God will go to save us from ourselves and from the disunity, disease, destruction, and dissolution that otherwise mark human history. The Reign of God, therefore, is the antidote on every level—from the individual and personal to the corporate and communal—to "the ways of the world" then, in the meanwhile, now, and for the future.

2. The Kingdom and the Church

If Jesus Christ as the proclaimer and embodiment of the Reign of God is the central burden of the Gospels, the rest of the New Testament is concerned, first, with how that fact got carried into the larger world beyond Palestine (Acts) and, second, how the church is to live in the world to which the "good news" of God's Reign is addressed (the Epistles). Among the various images employed as icons of the church in those writings, the Body of Christ is predominant, especially in, but not limited to, the Pauline epistles. The early church declared those writings "apostolic," that is, consistent with the missional message of the "sent ones" (Apostles) in regard to the Reign of God / Kingdom God.

Constituted by its members as the Body of Christ through baptism and receiving thereby the Holy Spirit's energizing gifts, the church is called in its life and mission to witness to the Reign of God / Kingdom of God. The central purpose of the church's witness is, therefore, to proclaim by word and action the values, signs, and accessibility of that Reign / Kingdom. All of this "good news" is joyfully received and nourished in the church for such

---

8. In order of appearance, Scripture citations are: Matthew 6:27 and Luke 16:13, John 5:6 and Mark 12:24.

a mission. This "gift" is continually replenished not only in the Eucharist, but by eucharistic living, whether personally and individually or corporately and communally.

3. Advent: Beginning the Year with Its End in Mind

The church's worship pattern of praise, attending to Scripture, intercession, repentance, reconciliation, and communion with the Triune God provides a weekly renewal and replenishment in our mission. A greater instrument, incorporating the weekly pattern and enlarging its significance, is found in the sanctification of all time by the seasons of the liturgical year. The year begins, of course, with Advent, and its principal focus is the Reign of God / Kingdom of Christ as found in the appointed Scripture readings.[9]

In an important sense, the annual round of the liturgical year picks up just where the New Testament concludes. There, appropriately, in the Book of Revelation, the central focus and methods of both Gospels and Epistles are disclosed. The solitary cry of consummation ("It is finished!") from Jesus's cross finds more than an echo in the proclamation of the cosmic Christ:

> The kingdoms of this world have become the Kingdom of our Lord, and of his Christ; and he shall reign for ever and ever.[10] See I am making all things new. It is done! I am the Alpha and the Omega, the beginning and the end.[11]

By venerable custom at the beginning of the secular new year there is a very human habit of reflecting on the year past and looking forward to the year ahead. Often this is accompanied by resolves to be better in some way or to do things differently. The hopeful atmosphere and practice of such resolutions is also by human habit often soon forgotten or dashed by the distractions and depredations of a world totally *un*-resolved to change its ways.

But for Christians at the beginning of a new liturgical year, our hope and our help, not to say our motivation and our mission, are rooted elsewhere.

---

9. The establishment of this fact was the burden of Chapter 1. The readings from the first Sunday after All Saints' Day until the last week of Advent are relentlessly eschatological, that is, directed to the Kingdom and not toward Bethlehem (incarnational) until the last week, but even then the birth of Jesus is put into eschatological perspective.

10. Revelation 11:15 (KJV). Readers are encouraged to hear Handel's "Hallelujah Chorus" from *The Messiah* in their heads!

11. Revelation 21:5–6 (NRSV). Note: Jesus's final cry of victory from the cross occurs only in John 19:30.

By framing the entire liturgical year from the beginning in an eschatological mode, we are encouraged to enter the annual round not simply as repeating a cyclic routine, but to engage each new year with Advent "eyes" that look to higher expectations, seek deeper understandings, and view broader horizons *in*, *with*, and *for* the Reign of God / Kingdom of Christ.[12] In short, we participate in the mission of that reality (our business) while awaiting its full manifestation (God's business).

4. Focus on Stewardship: Bringing It All Together

There have been hints all along the way of this short discussion about the relationship between the Reign / Kingdom of God and stewardship. As characterized in the previous section, an expanded Advent appears at the beginning of the ecclesiastical year as exactly the appropriate season for the annual address to ourselves about stewardship. First of all, generous living on the pattern of the Triune God as disclosed in the life and mission of Jesus Christ seems obvious. Secondly, if, to use the customary words, our "time, talents, and treasure" are all a gift of such a Divinity, then living eucharistically, that is, thankfully, is our very *modus operandi* as Christians and as church.

We also know, as well, that stewardship is a larger concept than simply living up to the monetary tithe as the standard of giving with which we have been gifted from our Jewish roots. Money is not unimportant, however. It is our servant, our means toward accomplishing much else for the common good as well as for ourselves. More largely, stewardship means regarding everything through the focus of the Reign of God / Kingdom of Christ. It thus involves heeding the prophetic call to seek the welfare, not to say the flourishing, of the human community.[13] The condition of such flourishing as

---

12. As discussed in Chapter 1, "eschatology" is a large concept. In a Christian context it refers to "the end" in a number of ways, but principally as the full and final manifestation of God's reign. At times, whether in Scripture or subsequent history, eschatology has gotten confused or conflated with an "apocalypticism" focused on dire or dread occurrences or, in fact, a judgmental destruction of the physical creation at an end of time. It would seem, then, that eschatology is best taken "neat" without an admixture of apocalypticism.

13. Jeremiah 29:7 and throughout the prophetic tradition in both Testaments. The best recent discussions concerning the flourishing of the human community from the perspective of the Reign of God / Kingdom of Christ are to be found in two volumes by Miroslav Volf: *A Public Faith: Followers of Christ Should Serve the Common Good* (Grand Rapids, MI: Brazos Press, 2011) and *Flourishing: Why We Need Religion in a Globalized World* (New Haven: Yale University Press, 2015).

God intends requires on every level the reconciling stewardship of peace.[14] Finally, stewardship by its very nature means attending to the care of creation. As aspects of stewardship, the hallmarks of the Reign of God / Kingdom of Christ are justice, peace, and the integrity of creation. Addressing stewardship in an expanded Advent, then, is both a natural and a graceful opportunity.

Coincidence of All Saints' Sunday and Advent

As has been noted, the first Sunday of an expanded Advent occurs between November 5 and 12. Occasionally, there will be a year when All Saints' Sunday occurs on or between November 5 and November 7. This presents a problem primarily for Anglicans who more than any others tend to observe the Feast of All Saints on the Sunday following rather than the fixed November 1 feast day itself. This allowance was made explicit in "The Calendar of the Church Year" rubric permitting this accommodation (BCP 1979, 15 and the Canadian Book of Alternative Services, 15).

There are several possible approaches to resolving the problem presented by this occasional coincidence:

1. Keep All Saints' Sunday the first Sunday of November and ignore the expanded Advent.

2. Begin an expanded Advent on the first Sunday of November and ignore All Saints' Sunday (keeping the feast on its day, November 1).

3. Observe All Saints' Sunday by transferring it to the Sunday just prior to November 1 and begin Advent on the first Sunday in November (Note: This alternative will not work for Lutherans since the last Sunday in October is Reformation Sunday).[15]

---

14. "Seek peace and pursue it" (1 Peter 3:11). Most biblical scholars understand 1 Peter to be an eschatological sermon on the implications of baptism. In any case, it is a fascinating, not to say revelatory, experience to read 1 Peter in a single sitting with that ecclesial context in one's imagination.

15. As one of the architects of full communion between Lutherans and Episcopalians (Lutheran-Episcopal Dialogue II and III, 1978–1991), and later a member of the Anglican-Lutheran International Commission (1993–2011), I can attest to the shock it causes when Lutherans realize that Episcopalians in particular and Anglicans generally do not observe Reformation Sunday. While not ultimately an impediment to full communion, this fact was at least a matter of concern requiring extensive explanation from Anglicans over the years.

4. Observe All Saints' Sunday exclusively on the first Sunday after November 1, and begin the expanded Advent with its second Sunday.

5. Plan a blended service on the Sunday following November 1, where the change from the All Saints focus to the beginning of the Advent season occurs within the liturgy.

Obviously, alternatives 1 and 2 are *not* to be commended. Alternative 3 is a viable possibility, the more so as the fixed feast of All Saints is closer half the time in those years when a coincidence arises. The fourth alternative, of course, compromises the expanded Advent season. This leaves the last possibility. Such a blended service is not unknown in the tradition.[16]

While the Advent Project Seminar commends the third alternative above, our fifth alternative is strongly recommended. To this end an *ordo* for a blended liturgy is provided here. Though this *ordo* is clearly based on Rite II of the Book of Common Prayer 1979, it may be easily adapted to any liturgy using the four-fold pattern of worship.

Suggested Ordo for an Advent 1 / All Saints' Sunday Liturgy

Prior to the liturgy the Paschal candle is lit for All Saints (and later the first candle of the Advent wreath set in its accustomed place is lit from it later in the service). The Feast of All Saints or All Saints' Sunday is one of the major days appointed for baptisms and that is taken into account.

Gathering Rite

Acclamation: first choice ("Kingdom") with baptismal additions
Hymn of Praise: for example "For All the Saints" (H82, # 287)
Procession of sanctuary party; *asperges* over the people
Salutation and Collect of the Day (All Saints' Day collect)

---

16. The transition of mood in one major liturgy is, furthermore, far more dramatic on "The Sunday of the Passion: Palm Sunday" than would be the case in an Advent 1 / All Saints liturgy. There is a massive shift in mood and focus between the palm ceremony rehearsing Jesus's triumphal entry into Jerusalem and the introduction to the solemnity of Holy Week represented by the Passion narrative occurring within a single liturgy.

Liturgy of the Word

Year A	Year B	Year C
Revelation 7:9–17	Wisdom 3:1–9	Daniel 7:1-3, 15–18
Psalm 34:1–10, 22	Psalm 24	Psalm 149:1–5
1 John 3:1–3	Revelation 21:1–6	Ephesians 1:11–23

Gospel Procession Hymn: for example,
"By All Your Saints Still Striving" (H82, # 231/232)

Matthew 5:1–12	John 11:32–44	Luke 6:20–31

Sermon / Homily

This is the obvious place to bring the themes of the two strands of the liturgy together at midpoint, that is, in communion with "the great cloud of witnesses," we are called to participate in manifesting God's reign of justice, peace, and care for creation.

Baptism / Renewal of Baptismal Covenant

Prayers of the People and Exchange of the Peace

*Nearly any form of the Prayers can be adapted to include both strands of this day. The one found in plenary form in Chapter 4: "Resources" is recommended here. The Prayers should conclude with the Collect for Advent 1(Sapientia / Wisdom) to be found also in the same chapter. **Note:** Prior to the Peace, the prayer of blessing (cf. Chapter 4) over the Advent wreath is said, during which water used in the opening Asperges may also be sprinkled on the wreath as a sign of blessing. After this, the first candle of the wreath is lighted with a flame taken from the Paschal candle.*

Liturgy of the Table

Offertory Hymn: for example, "Lo! He Comes with Clouds
Descending" (H82, # 57)
Sursum corda, First Proper Preface of Advent, *Sanctus* and
Benedictus
The Great Thanksgiving: Prayer B (BCP, 1979) and Lord's Prayer

Breaking of the Bread and Holy Communion
Communion Hymn: for example, "Let All Mortal Flesh Keep
  Silence" (H82, # 324)

Sending Rite

Either of two sending prayers (BCP 1979) following communion
Blessing (*cf.* Chapter 4 above: Blessing for an Expanded Advent)
Sending Hymn: for example, "Prepare the Way, O Zion" (H82, # 65)
Dismissal[17]

Church / Sunday School in an Expanded Advent

Integrating the observance of an expanded Advent into the church or Sunday school of any congregation will, of course, be greatly aided if the curriculum in use follows the liturgical year and, more importantly, is keyed to the lectionary. With regard to this latter point, the focus for any given Sunday will then be congruent with the readings that form the Liturgy of the Word for the entire worshiping community. This, in turn, raises questions of whether adult education is conducted concomitantly with church or Sunday school at a time before or after worship or whether the children are in class during all or part of the main Sunday liturgy. It would seem that no one pattern can fit every situation.

The approach to the questions involved, therefore, will be anecdotal and concern a parish where an expanded Advent has been observed for some years. Clergy and directors of Christian education in congregations can then

---

17. The basic idea for a blended service and first drafting of its shape is to be credited to an original member of the Advent Project Seminar. Dr. Jill Burnett Comings served for many years as director of research for the seminar. She has been an assistant professor of liturgical studies at Drew University (Methodist), and has taught at the General Theological Seminary in New York (Episcopal) as well as the School of Theology and Ministry in Seattle University (Roman Catholic).

One of her major insights as a scholar of liturgical history is to view All Saints' Day as itself a transition from the old to the new liturgical year, especially with its emphasis on the communion of saints in the Body of Christ. For a *précis* of Dr. Coming's paper "Culmination in the *Communio Sanctorum*: Celebrating the Feast of All Saints as the Completion of the Liturgical Year," see *Proceedings* (Notre Dame, IN: NAAL, Inc., 2010), 36. Furthermore, when the Feast of Christ the King was originally established by Pope Pius XI in 1925 he specifically placed it on the last Sunday of October "because it is at the end of the liturgical year," that is, the Sunday before All Saints' Day (*Quas primas*, 13; also see Chapter 3, footnote 22 for full reference).

glean from the experience of others how their participation in trial usage of a longer season might be integrated into their setting. This particular narrative recounts a visit by my wife and me to one such parish and reflects not only observation through participation in the liturgy, but conversation with the rector, the family minister, and one of the Sunday school teachers.[18]

St. Gabriel the Archangel Episcopal Church has a worship space that is semi-circularly arranged around a free-standing altar with tall clear windows behind, keeping the entire church well-lighted during the daytime. The first three rows in the nave are comprised of flexible seating (which is removed after the liturgy and replaced with tables for post-worship social time). The raised platform that defines the sanctuary or altar area featured a seven candle Advent wreath (six blue and a central white one) placed to the congregation's left. The choir singing from the left side of the congregation effectively supported the assembly's Advent hymnody and they sang an offertory anthem as well.

The particular Sunday was a busy one with baptisms and confirmations during the bishop of Oregon's visitation. In a word, the church was packed and the observance of *Oriens* Sunday was enthusiastic even in the face of the fact that the actual morning star was completely occluded and it was pouring rain outside! Later we discovered in conversation with the bishop that through effective and engaging leadership of its rector, the parish has moved over the past few years from nearly moribund to active and growing, attracting many families with children, though maintaining a broad age-range.

Excepting babies and toddlers in the nursery, the Sunday school children normally come into the nave to join their parents for the Liturgy of the Table and Sending Rite. On this day, however, with baptisms and confirmations, the children were present and participating for the whole liturgy. Having been introduced during post-liturgy announcements, we were recipients during a splendid buffet reception of many enthusiastic comments from parishioners about the experience of an expanded Advent. Since the liturgical year forms a basis of the curriculum in this parish, the children's church

---

18. In order of mention: The Rev. LouAnn Pickering, Page Clothier, and Evelyn Schoop. Schoop is also a freelance writer and had, in fact, just published an article on the spirituality of an expanded Advent in the December 2015 number of *The Atlantic* magazine entitled, "One Christian Family's Antidote to the Christmas Frenzy," (http://www.theatlantic.com/business/archives/2015/12/advent-christmas-calm/421515).

school time effectively formed the Liturgy of the Word for them.

In extended conversation with the lay family minister, we learned that this was the first year that the whole congregation had been observing an expanded Advent. With her encouragement, the church school had been observing the longer Advent for two years previously. Families had been drawn in through activities that the children were doing (for example, bringing home a seven-candle Advent wreath and prayers modeled on the season's seven collects). Church school stories and activities had been focused on the children's creation for the congregation of a Jesse Tree exhibiting Jesus's lineage and also the Messianic titles of the Great "O" antiphons.

The unanticipated approach at St. Gabriel's appeared to be the fulfillment of the Scripture, "a little child shall lead them" (Isaiah 11:6)! More often the question has been put in terms of what to do with the church or Sunday school after the observance of an expanded Advent has come under consideration as a possibility. This strategy of reversing the usual, however, has that typical scriptural, not to say subversive, flair reflected in any number of instances of choosing seemingly unlikely persons for leadership roles (for example, from the young David as God's choice, to the twelve apostles selected by Jesus from the disciples, to Saul the persecutor who became Paul the apostle). In any case, in this instance the church school children became heralds of a liturgical year renewed at its inception.

Here, then, is a suggestion. Let the church or Sunday school children be involved during the first three weeks of an expanded Advent with stories around the characters in Jesus's lineage (some will, of course, be shocking, but that's the nature of Scripture, too) and individually work on projects exemplifying those stories. Collectively, the church or Sunday school could be involved with creating a Jesse Tree for presentation to the congregation later in Advent. Meanwhile, during Advent's early weeks the church or Sunday school could also be involved with producing a pageant based on these themes to be presented on the fourth Sunday early in December, that is, *Radix Jesse* (Root of Jesse) Sunday.[19]

---

19. When I expressed this idea to a colleague, she responded playfully questioning whether there might not be a casting problem: would there be a rush to play Rahab in an Advent pageant comparable to the competition to play Mary in a Christmas pageant? Rahab is, of course, exactly one of those unlikely persons in salvation history

This proposal might, however, have a doubly heuristic effect, at once replacing a too-early children's Christmas pageant and taking the pressure off church school leaders from producing a

The purpose of this brief narrative has been to stimulate imagination and to show what can happen when people think creatively about a particular concern in regard to our general subject. As indicated, no general pattern is applicable, but at least one congregation has led the way in imagining how an expanded Advent and church or Sunday school can be effectively related. This, perhaps, provides just the transition needed to the final section of this chapter and, indeed, of the book itself.

Congregational / Parish Participation

If, by virtue of the author's tradition, this book has come out of an Anglican perspective in general and more particularly from a priest and professor in the Episcopal Church, its scope both historically and presently has been ecumenical in intention and exhibition. This range across traditions is reflective of a half-century career that has involved a wide spectrum not only of liturgical but ecumenical involvements on the local, national, and international levels of ecclesial life. On the basis of such experience, it is a given that the adoption by congregations or parishes of a trial usage of an expanded Advent proposed in this book must take into account the differing polities exhibited by various traditions. To sharpen the question, how or by what authority can this be undertaken?

For churches with a more congregational polity a decision by pastors, church musicians, and worship commissions can suffice to authorize entry into trial usage.[20] Having made the decision they can then prepare the congregation through newsletters, website posts, and two or three educational sessions in early autumn for the initiation of an expanded Advent observance. The Advent Project Seminar hopes that the leadership of congregations new to the observance will be in touch with us through our website, not only to find resources beyond those already set forth in this book, but also for the pur-

---

still-inappropriate late-Advent Christmas one. Some congregations, in fact, have begun moving the Christmas pageant altogether from an Advent location and have put it on or near Epiphany as the culmination of the Twelve Days when the Matthean magi finally appear to complement the Lukan shepherds of the Christmas Eve gospel reading.

20. Besides piquing the interest of clergy, the Advent Project Seminar has discovered that church musicians in particular have been quick to see the possibilities of an expanded Advent in creating time and space for advancing the congregation's exposure to the rich array of Advent music that in a truncated season often goes neglected.

pose of evaluating the experience afterward. The Advent Project Seminar has been collecting and collating such evaluations for over a decade and they have helped us further refine our work in service of the church's life and mission.

Other parishes, such as those in the Episcopal Church or the Anglican Church of Canada, will first have to seek permission to enter into trial usage of an expanded Advent from their bishop in his or her capacity as the chief liturgical officer of the diocese. Clergy whose interest has been piqued can be in touch through the Advent Project Seminar and we will provide an initial supporting letter to bishops explaining the project and seconding the parish request for permission to enter into such trial usage.[21] We normally ask all congregations for a three-year commitment for two reasons. First of all, three years of an expanded Advent exposes the congregation to one full cycle of the three-year lectionary. Second, there is enough challenge to culturally-based customs in some aspects of the project to make a single year's experience insufficient for effective evaluation. The Advent Project Seminar has, for instance, seen initial "so-so" or even negative evaluations move over three years to a very positive, "What are we waiting for!"

Much depends, however, on the care taken to introduce the project to the congregation. In this regard, I am reminded of my time on the liturgical commission in the Diocese of California during the early years of trial usage leading to the 1979 Book of Common Prayer. We received site reports where, in effect, the priest told the congregation, "General Convention has authorized these new rites for trial usage and I know you're not going to like them, but the bishop says we have to try them out." With such introductions, we were not amazed to discover that those parishes did not favor the new rites. No one, however, is under any compulsion with this project. It is, rather, completely invitational.

The discussion of polity to this point leaves us, of course, with the largest of the liturgical churches. Whether or to what degree this proposal can be comprehended by the polity of the Roman Catholic Church is a major consideration. It is precisely here that I must turn to a story rather than to an assessment of juridical possibilities or impossibilities. From 2010 through

---

21. The Advent Project Seminar has been encouraged by the growing number of bishops in the Episcopal Church and the Anglican Church of Canada who have enthusiastically extended such permission to parishes. Seminar members have also responded to requests for diocesan-wide presentations of the project through general workshops or conferences with diocesan liturgical commissions.

2016 I served by appointment of our presiding bishop as the Episcopal Church's representative to the Consultation on Common Texts.[22] CCT is the custodian and publisher of the *Revised Common Lectionary* and other ecumenical texts for worship. This body, which meets annually, is comprised of representatives from twenty-six churches in the United States and Canada, including official representatives of the national Council of Catholic Bishops in those two countries.

At its annual meeting, CCT sponsors a day-long public forum on a relevant topic, inviting participation of a wide ecumenical range of local church leaders from that year's venue. The April 2012 forum in the metropolitan New York City area consisted of a presentation and workshop by members of the Advent Project. All of this set the scene for CCT's review and evaluation of the forum on the second day of our meeting. Overall the comments of church representatives were positive and the questions addressed to me and the other Advent Project Seminar members were supportive and helpful to our further development of the project. The growing ecumenical scope of the project was particularly a matter of interest to the CCT representatives. However, the proverbial "elephant in the room" concerned the possibility of Roman Catholic participation in any way short of an unlikely official permission from the Vatican Congregation for Divine Worship. Hence, the "whether and to what degree" question mentioned above.

As the review and evaluation session continued, one of the Roman Catholic representatives, himself a liturgical theologian, said, "Well, Bill, we're not likely to see any calendar reform in our lifetime, but I don't see why some elements of the proposal can't be used in our parishes." After that remarkable statement, general discussion continued by enumerating what those elements might be. Short of naming an expanded Advent, among them were:

- Highlighting that the eschatological lectionary (OLM) is already in place over the seven weeks;

- Noting that an expanded season is not unknown (for example, Milan);

22. After 2016 I have continued on CCT as a member-at-large. During my tenure as the Episcopal Church's representative I also served, along with a colleague from the United Church of Canada, as a CCT representative to the international and ecumenical English Language Liturgical Consultation, which meets biennially at the venue for that year of *Societas Liturgica*, the international and ecumenical academy of liturgical theologians.

106

- Encouraging homilies in the seven weeks focused on the formation of an eschatological character;

- Employing the resources of Advent music in the seven week period.

All of these items could be set forth through the usual means of communication in diocese or parishes. They are not intended as subversive of liturgical authority, but as a renewal based on already authorized resources within the Roman Catholic Church. In addition, a great deal of the documentation of this book has drawn upon scholars and liturgical theologians of the Roman Catholic Church. In any case the Advent Project Seminar invites such participation of parishes to the degree that it is possible and would be delighted to receive reflections and evaluations from any parishes that become aware of this proposal for renewal as focused on eschatological formation at a crucial juncture in the liturgical year.

Conclusion and Commencement

It seems more than fitting to conclude a particular proposal for liturgical renewal on an ecumenical note. As Christians, we can no longer afford—if ever we could have—to expend energy on the maintenance of our erstwhile hard-won divisions. Especially in today's world we face immense challenges. It is a world, moreover, where the means of communication have become instantaneously global while people have less and less to say that really makes for the flourishing of the human community or the common good. The burden of this book has, in the face of such a situation, a very limited purpose. It offers not so much a solution as it proposes a context for Christian traditions without which we cannot faithfully exhibit or live out our participation in the Reign of God / Kingdom of Christ. Such participation aims in every way toward justice, peace, and the integrity of creation as precisely the hallmarks of that Reign / Kingdom.

In our worship we celebrate the values of that Reign of God / Kingdom of Christ to the end that we may more deeply appropriate them for their demonstration as we relate to others, not only as individuals, but as a community of faith with a mission. That mission is the flourishing of the human community from a divine perspective rooted in a costly, but generous creation-renewing and life-giving love, perhaps best summed up for us in this prayer:

Lord Jesus Christ, you stretched out your arms of love on the hard wood of the cross that everyone might come within the reach of your saving embrace: So clothe us in your Spirit that we, reaching forth our hands in love, may bring those who do not know you to the knowledge and love of you; for the honor of your name. *Amen.*[23]

The commencement aspect of this conclusion has to do with the particular proposal for liturgical renewal itself. Compelling reasons in our time for a re-imagined Advent season have been asserted in this study along with the delineation of Scriptural and other resources available for an expanded Advent. In consideration of the very liminality of Advent, it begs to be freed from the cultural fetters of its present truncated form. The longer time for the season is required for an effective eschatological formation of the church's life and mission. And, at the commencement of each new liturgical year, it is this formation that is not only the emphasis of Advent, but the very character that must be carried into the entire liturgical year. So framed by an expanded Advent at its inception, the entire liturgical year can be freed *from* routine repetition and *for* the hope of engaging the year with ever higher expectations, deeper understandings, and broader horizons *in, with,* and *for* the Reign of God / Kingdom of Christ.

---

23. Third collect for mission (particularly suited to Fridays), BCP 1979, 101. The prayer was composed by Bishop Charles Henry Brent (1862–1929), bishop of the Philippines and then of Western New York and founder of the Faith and Order Movement (1927) that later merged with Life and Work to form the World Council of Churches in 1948.

Bibliography

Reference Works

Book of Alternative Services of the Anglican Church of Canada. Toronto, ON: The Anglican Book Center, 1985.

Book of Blessings. Collegeville, MN: Order of St. Benedict, Inc., 1989.

Book of Common Prayer 1979. New York: Church Publishing, 1979.

Book of Common Prayer 1928. New York: Church Hymnal Corporation, 1952.

Book of Common Worship. Louisville, KY: Westminster/John Knox Press, 1993.

Book of Occasional Services. New York: Church Publishing, 2004.

Book of Worship. Nashville, TN: United Methodist Publishing House, 1992.

Common Praise being the Hymnal of the Anglican Church of Canada. Toronto: The Anglican Book Centre, 1998.

Companion to the Hymnal 1982. Four volumes. Edited by Raymond E. Glover. New York: Church Hymnal Corporation, 1994.

Documents of Vatican II. Edited by Walter M. Abbott, S.J. New York: The America Press, 1966.

Encyclopedia of Theology. The Concise Sacramentum Mundi. Edited by Karl Rahner. New York: The Seabury Press, 1975.

Evangelical Lutheran Worship. Minneapolis, MN: Augsburg-Fortress, 2006.

Greek-English Lexicon of the New Testament and Other Early Christian Literature. Edited by William F. Arndt and F. Wilbur Gingrich. Chicago University Press, 1952.

Interpreter's Dictionary of the Bible: An Illustrated Encyclopedia in Four Volumes. Nashville: Abingdon Press, 1962.

Lectionary for the Mass. Volume 1: *Sundays, Solemnities, Feasts of the Lord and the Saints (OLM)*. Study Edition. Collegeville, MN: The Liturgical Press, 1998.

Oxford Book of Medieval English Verse. Edited by Celia and Kenneth Sisam. Oxford: Clarendon Press, 1970.

Oxford Dictionary of the Christian Church. 3rd edition. New York: Oxford University Press, 1997.

The Hymnal 1982. New York: Church Publishing, 1985.

Roman Missal. 3rd edition, English Translation. Washington, DC: United States Conference of Catholic Bishops, 2011.

The Revised Common Lectionary. 20th Anniversary Annotated Edition. Minneapolis, MN: Fortress Press, 2012.

Monographs and Articles

Alexander, Neil. *Celebrating Liturgical Time: Days, Weeks, and Seasons.* New York: Church Publishing, 2014.

Augustine. *The City of God.* Modern Library Edition by Marcus Dods. New York: Random House, Inc., 1994.

Bradshaw, Paul F. and Maxwell E. Johnson. *The Origins of Feasts, Fasts, and Seasons in Early Christianity.* Collegeville, MN: Liturgical Press, 2011.

"Constitution on the Sacred Liturgy," *Documents of Vatican II.* Edited by Walter M. Abbott, S.J. New York: The America Press, 1966.

Crossan, John Dominic. *God and Empire: Jesus Against Rome, Then and Now.* New York: Harper, 2007.

———. *The Power of Parable: How Fiction by Jesus Became Fiction about Jesus.* New York: HarperOne, 2012.

———. *How to Read the Bible and Still Be a Christian: Struggling with Divine Violence from Genesis through Revelation.* New York: HarperOne, 2015.

Dante, Alighieri. *The Divine Comedy: 1 Hell.* Translation and Commentary by Dorothy. L. Sayers. New York: Penguin Books, 1949.

De Clerck, Paul. "The Liturgical Reform of Vatican II: Why Has It Only Been Partially Received?" *Worship.* Volume 88:2. Collegeville, MN: Liturgical Press, 2014.

John Donne. Edited by John Hayward. Baltimore: The Penguin Poets, 1960.

Joustra, Robert and Alissa Wilkinson. *How to Survive the Apocalypse: Zombies, Cylons, Faith, and Politics at the End of the World.* Grand Rapids, MI: Eerdmans, 2016.

Larson-Miller, Lizette. "Consuming Time," *Worship.* Volume 88:6. Collegeville, MN: Liturgical Press, 2014.

McKinnon, James. *The Advent Project: The Later-Seventh Century Creation of the Roman Mass Proper.* Berkeley: University of California Press, 2000.

Malloy, Patrick. *Celebrating the Eucharist: A Practical Guide for Clergy and Other Liturgical Ministers.* New York: Church Publishing, 2007.

Maurice, F. D. *The Kingdom of Christ.* London: James Clarke & Co., 1959.

———. *Theological Essays.* NY: Harper & Brothers, Publishers, 1957.

Meyers, Ruth A. *Missional Worship and Worshipful Mission: Gathering as God's People, Going Out in God's Name.* Grand Rapids, MI: William B. Eerdmans Publishing Company, 2014.

O'Connell, Martin. *Eternity Today: On the Liturgical Year.* Volume 1: *God and Time: Advent, Christmas, Epiphany.* New York: Continuum Press, 2006.

O'Donnell, Emma. *Remembering the Future: The Experience of Time in Jewish and Christian Liturgy.* Collegeville, MN: Liturgical Press, 2015.

Oliver, Mary. *THIRST.* Boston: Beacon Press, 2006.

Pope Pius XI. *Quas primas.* English Translation. http://w2.vatican.va/content/piusxi-/en/encyclicals/documents/hf_p-xi_enc_11121925_quas_primas.html.

Rausch, Thomas, S.J. *Eschatology, Liturgy, and Christology.* Collegeville, MN: Liturgical Press, 2012.

Rossing, Barbara R. *The Rapture Exposed: The Message of Hope in the Book of Revelation.* Boulder, CO: Westview Press, 2004.

Schmemann, Alexander. *Introduction to Liturgical Theology.* Crestwood, NY: St. Vladimir's Seminary Press, 1966.

———. *For the Life of the World: Sacraments and Orthodoxy.* 2nd edition. Crestwood, NY: St. Vladimir's Seminary Press, 1973.

Schoop, Evelyn, "One Christian Family's Antidote to the Christmas Frenzy," *The Atlantic*, December 2015.

Shepherd, Massey H., Jr. *The Oxford American Prayer Book Commentary.* New York: Oxford University Press, 1963.

Smith, James K. A. *Desiring the Kingdom: Worship, Worldview, and Cultural Formation.* Grand Rapids, MI: Baker Academic, 2009.

————. *Imagining the Kingdom: How Worship Works*. Grand Rapids, MI: Baker Academic, 2013.

Smith, Pamela Grenfell. "Let Advent Go." http://www.baba-yaga.org.

Talley, Thomas J. *The Origin of the Liturgical Year*. Collegeville, MN: Liturgical Press, 1986.

Volf, Miroslav. *A Public Faith: How Followers of Christ Should Serve the Common Good*. Grand Rapids, MI: Brazos Press, 2011.

————. *Flourishing: Why We Need Religion in a Globalized World*. New Haven: Yale University Press, 2015.

Von Balthasar, Hans Urs. *The Glory of the Lord: A Theological Aesthetics*. Volume 7: *The New Covenant*. Translated by Brian McNeil. San Francisco: Ignatius Press, 1989.

Wilbricht, Stephen S. *Rehearsing God's Just Kingdom: The Eucharistic Vision of Mark Searle*. Collegeville, MN: The Liturgical Press, 2013.